Weather and Climate Inventory
National Park Service
Chihuahuan Desert Network

Natural Resource Technical Report NPS/CHDN/NRTR—2007/034
WRCC Report 2007-09

Christopher A. Davey, Kelly T. Redmond, and David B. Simeral
Western Regional Climate Center
Desert Research Institute
2215 Raggio Parkway
Reno, Nevada 89512-1095

May 2007

U.S. Department of the Interior
National Park Service
Natural Resource Program Center
Fort Collins, Colorado

The Natural Resource Publication series addresses natural resource topics that are of interest and applicability to a broad readership in the National Park Service and to others in the management of natural resources, including the scientific community, the public, and the National Park Service conservation and environmental constituencies. Manuscripts are peer-reviewed to ensure that the information is scientifically credible, technically accurate, appropriately written for the intended audience, and designed and published in a professional manner.

The Natural Resources Technical Reports series is used to disseminate the peer-reviewed results of scientific studies in the physical, biological, and social sciences for both the advancement of science and the achievement of the National Park Service mission. The reports provide contributors with a forum for displaying comprehensive data that are often deleted from journals because of page limitations. Current examples of such reports include the results of research that address natural resource management issues; natural resource inventory and monitoring activities; resource assessment reports; scientific literature reviews; and peer-reviewed proceedings of technical workshops, conferences, or symposia.

Views and conclusions in this report are those of the authors and do not necessarily reflect policies of the National Park Service. Mention of trade names or commercial products does not constitute endorsement or recommendation for use by the National Park Service.

Printed copies of reports in these series may be produced in a limited quantity and they are only available as long as the supply lasts. This report is also available from the Natural Resource Publications Management website (http://www.nature.nps.gov/publications/NRPM) on the Internet or by sending a request to the address on the back cover.

Please cite this publication as follows:

Davey, C. A., K. T. Redmond, and D. B. Simeral. 2007. Weather and Climate Inventory, National Park Service, Chihuahuan Desert Network. Natural Resource Technical Report NPS/CHDN/NRTR—2007/034. National Park Service, Fort Collins, Colorado.

NPS/CHDN/NRTR—2007/034, May 2007

Contents

Contents (continued)

Figures

Tables

Appendixes

Acronyms

AASC	American Association of State Climatologists
ACIS	Applied Climate Information System
AMIS	Amistad National Recreation Area
ASOS	Automated Surface Observing System
AWOS	Automated Weather Observing System
BIBE	Big Bend National Park
BLM	Bureau of Land Management
CASTNet	Clean Air Status and Trends Network
CAVE	Carlsbad Caverns National Park
CHDN	Chihuahuan Desert Inventory and Monitoring Network
COOP	Cooperative Observer Program
CRN	Climate Reference Network
CWOP	Citizen Weather Observer Program
DFIR	Double-Fence Intercomparison Reference
DST	daylight savings time
ENSO	El Niño Southern Oscillation
EPA	Environmental Protection Agency
FAA	Federal Aviation Administration
FODA	Fort Davis National Historic Site
FIPS	Federal Information Processing Standards
GMT	Greenwich Mean Time
GOES	Geostationary Operational Environmental Satellite
GPMP	NPS Gaseous Pollutant Monitoring Program
GPS	Global Positioning System
GPS-MET	NOAA ground-based GPS meteorology
GUMO	Guadalupe Mountains National Park
I&M	NPS Inventory and Monitoring Program
LEO	Low Earth Orbit
LST	local standard time
LTER	Long Term Ecological Research
MDN	Mercury Deposition Network
NADP	National Atmospheric Deposition Program
NAMS	North American Monsoon System
NASA	National Aeronautics and Space Administration
NCDC	National Climatic Data Center
NetCDF	Network Common Data Form
NOAA	National Oceanic and Atmospheric Administration
NPS	National Park Service
NRCS	Natural Resources Conservation Service
NWS	National Weather Service
PRISM	Parameter Regression on Independent Slopes Model
RAWS	Remote Automated Weather Station network
RCC	regional climate center
RIGR	Rio Grande Wild and Scenic River

SAO	Surface Airways Observation network
Surfrad	Surface Radiation Budget network
SNOTEL	Snowfall Telemetry network
SOD	Summary Of the Day
USDA	U.S. Department of Agriculture
USGS	U.S. Geological Survey
UTC	Coordinated Universal Time
WBAN	Weather Bureau Army Navy
WHSA	White Sands National Monument
WMO	World Meteorological Organization
WRCC	Western Regional Climate Center
WX4U	Weather For You network

Executive Summary

Climate is a dominant factor driving the physical and ecologic processes affecting the Chihuahuan Desert Inventory and Monitoring Network (CHDN). The CHDN region has a relatively uniform climate spatially and is generally characterized as a cold desert, with hot summers and cool to cold, dry winters. Precipitation in the CHDN generally is convective in nature and associated with monsoonal rains during the summer months, especially in the Chihuahuan Desert ecoregion. This precipitation drives pulses of water inputs that strongly influence the spatial distribution of CHDN ecosystems. Drought has been one of the principal historical sources of disturbance in the CHDN, limiting seedling establishment and productivity and driving wildfire frequency and intensity. Climate change is an issue of much concern for the CHDN. Of all the possible effects of future climate changes across the CHDN, global warming in particular is viewed as a likely future threat to the integrity of park ecosystems. Such changes may affect vegetation at the individual, population, or community level and precipitate changes in ecosystem function and structure, with corresponding management concerns. Because of its influence on the ecology of CHDN park units and the surrounding areas, climate was identified as a high-priority vital sign for CHDN and is one of the 12 basic inventories to be completed for all National Park Service (NPS) Inventory and Monitoring Program (I&M) networks.

This project was initiated to inventory past and present climate monitoring efforts in the CHDN. In this report, we provide the following information:

- Overview of broad-scale climatic factors and zones important to CHDN park units.
- Inventory of weather and climate station locations in and near CHDN park units relevant to the NPS I&M Program.
- Results of an inventory of metadata on each weather station, including affiliations for weather-monitoring networks, types of measurements recorded at these stations, and information about the actual measurements (length of record, etc.).
- Initial evaluation of the adequacy of coverage for existing weather stations and recommendations for improvements in monitoring weather and climate.

The CHDN has more precipitation compared to other nearby desert ecoregions, with annual precipitation averaging above 200 mm across the network. In central and western portions of CHDN, topography plays a major role in defining the spatial distribution of precipitation, while to the east, precipitation is inversely proportional to distance from the Gulf Coast. Mean annual precipitation totals vary from well under 200 mm in lower elevations of western CHDN park units to around 500 mm in Amistad National Recreation Area (AMIS). Much of the precipitation in the CHDN falls during the months of July to September, associated primarily with monsoon thunderstorm activity. Mean annual temperatures across the CHDN vary largely as a function of elevation, increasing from the northwest to the southeast. These temperatures range from below 12°C at higher elevations of Guadalupe Mountains National Park (GUMO) to over 20°C at AMIS. January minimum temperatures in the CHDN are generally near or below freezing (0°C) except along the Rio Grande, while July maximum temperatures get well above 30°C along portions of the Rio Grande. Interannual climate variations across the CHDN region are driven strongly by interannual variations in the intensity of the summer monsoonal flow and by variations in ENSO (El Niño Southern Oscillation). Little if any discernible trend can be noted in precipitation time series over the last century for the CHDN, while temperatures have shown warming, particularly in the last 2-3 decades.

Through a search of national databases and inquiries to NPS staff, we have identified 21 weather and climate stations within CHDN park units. Big Bend National Park (BIBE) has the most stations within park boundaries (13). Most weather and climate stations identified for the CHDN had metadata and data records that are sufficiently complete and satisfactory in quality.

The current coverage of weather/climate stations within much of the CHDN is unsatisfactory for ongoing ecological monitoring efforts. Precipitation in the CHDN desert locations is highly variable, both spatially and temporally. Unfortunately, very little data is available to permit a better understanding of these precipitation patterns. The weather/climate stations that have been identified are mostly located near visitor centers and other areas with higher visitor concentration. Very little coverage exists away from these locations. Sparse station coverage is also fairly common outside of the CHDN park units, forcing CHDN weather/climate monitoring efforts to sometimes look to distant sources (e.g. Indio Mountain Research Station) and even international sources (e.g. Mexico stations) for data.

Station coverage for Carlsbad Caverns National Park (CAVE) and GUMO is limited primarily to the visitor centers. Weather monitoring efforts could benefit greatly by installing one remote near-real-time station, such as a Remote Automated Weather Station (RAWS), in the western portions of both park units. This could be especially beneficial for GUMO, due to the greater heterogeneity of ecotypes within the park unit that currently lack weather/climate observations.

Like CAVE and GUMO, the weather/climate station identified at White Sands National Monument (WHSA) is situated near the main visitor center. As WHSA must rely heavily on outside sources of weather and climate data, climate monitoring efforts for WHSA will likely benefit by working with local agencies to encourage the continued operation of both long-term stations (e.g., Jornada Experimental Range) and near-real-time stations in the area.

With the exception of the Del Rio Airport, very little coverage of near-real-time stations exists in and around AMIS. If resources allow, AMIS may want to consider installing an automated station (such as RAWS) at Amistad Dam, to complement the existing Cooperative Observer Program (COOP) station. Another option would be to install an automated station along the Rio Grande near the western edge of AMIS, which would not only benefit weather monitoring efforts in AMIS, but also provide an eastern data point for monitoring near-real-time weather conditions along the Rio Grande Wild and Scenic River (RIGR). A western data point for RIGR could also be provided by installing a near-real-time station like RAWS at one of the existing COOP stations in BIBE (e.g., "Boquillas R.S." or "Castolon"). Near-real-time weather monitoring efforts in BIBE, which currently has little automated station coverage away from the main visitor centers (e.g., Chisos Basin and Panther Junction), could be greatly improved by adding such a station along the Rio Grande. By adding near-real-time stations at both the west and east ends of RIGR, some of the climate monitoring needs for RIGR could begin to be addressed while simultaneously keeping the main portion of RIGR free from additional man-made structures, in accordance with the mission of being a wild and scenic riverway.

Acknowledgements

This work was supported and completed under Task Agreement H8R07010001, with the Great Basin Cooperative Ecosystem Studies Unit. We would like to acknowledge very helpful assistance from various NPS personnel associated with the Chihuahuan Desert Inventory and Monitoring Network. Particular thanks are extended to Hildy Reiser and Tom Richie. We also thank John Gross, Margaret Beer, Grant Kelly, Greg McCurdy, and Heather Angeloff for all their help. Seth Gutman with the National Oceanic and Atmospheric Administration Earth Systems Research Laboratory provided valuable input on the GPS-MET station network. Portions of the work were supported by the NOAA Western Regional Climate Center.

1.0. Introduction

Weather and climate are key drivers in ecosystem structure and function. Global- and regional-scale climate variations will have a tremendous impact on natural systems (Chapin et al. 1996; Schlesinger 1997; Jacobson et al. 2000; Bonan 2002). Proper understanding of ecosystem dynamics requires an understanding of the roles of climate variability, hydrologic interactions with soils, and adaptive strategies of biota to capitalize on spatially and temporally variable moisture dynamics (Noy-Meir 1973; Bailey 1995; Rodriguez-Iturbe 2000; Reynolds et al. 2004). Long-term patterns in temperature and precipitation provide first-order constraints on potential ecosystem structure and function. Secondary constraints are realized from the intensity and duration of individual weather events and, additionally, from seasonality and inter-annual climate variability. These constraints influence the fundamental properties of ecologic systems, such as soil–water relationships, plant–soil processes, and nutrient cycling, as well as disturbance rates and intensity. These properties, in turn, influence the life-history strategies supported by a climatic regime (Neilson 1987; Reiser et al. 2006).

Given the importance of climate, it is one of 12 basic inventories to be completed by the National Park Service (NPS) Inventory and Monitoring Program (I&M) network (I&M 2006). As primary environmental drivers for the other vital signs, weather and climate patterns present various practical and management consequences and implications for the NPS (Oakley et al. 2003). Most park units observe weather and climate elements as part of their overall mission. The lands under NPS stewardship provide many excellent locations for monitoring climatic conditions.

It is essential that park units within the Chihuahuan Desert Inventory and Monitoring Network (CHDN) have an effective climate-monitoring system in place to track climate changes and to aid in management decisions relating to these changes. The purpose of this report is to determine the current status of weather and climate monitoring within the CHDN (Table 1.1; Figure 1.1). In this report, we provide the following informational elements:

- Overview of broad-scale climatic factors and zones important to CHDN park units.
- Inventory of locations for all weather stations in and near CHDN park units that are relevant to the NPS I&M networks.
- Results of metadata inventory for each station, including weather-monitoring network affiliations, types of recorded measurements, and information about actual measurements (length of record, etc.).
- Initial evaluation of the adequacy of coverage for existing weather stations and recommendations for improvements in monitoring weather and climate.

A primary question to be addressed by climate- and weather-monitoring activities in CHDN is as follows (Reiser et al. 2006):

- Are temperature and precipitation regimes changing over time (including timing, intensity, duration, and geographic distribution)?

1.1. Network Terminology

Before proceeding, it is important to stress that this report discusses the idea of "networks" in two different ways. Modifiers are used to distinguish between NPS I&M networks and weather/climate station networks. See Appendix A for a full definition of these terms.

Table 1.1. Park units in the Chihuahuan Desert Network.

Acronym	Name
AMIS	Amistad National Recreation Area
BIBE	Big Bend National Park
CAVE	Carlsbad Caverns National Park
FODA	Fort Davis National Historic Site
GUMO	Guadalupe Mountains National Park
RIGR	Rio Grande Wild and Scenic River
WHSA	White Sands National Monument

1.1.1. Weather/Climate Station Networks

Most weather and climate measurements are made not from isolated stations but from stations that are part of a network operated in support of a particular mission. The limiting case is a network of one station, where measurements are made by an interested observer or group. Larger networks usually have additional inventory data and station-tracking procedures. Some national weather/climate networks are associated with the National Oceanic and Atmospheric Administration (NOAA), including the National Weather Service (NWS) Cooperative Observer Program (COOP). Other national networks include the interagency Remote Automated Weather Station (RAWS) network and the U.S. Department of Agriculture/Natural Resources Conservation Service (USDA/NRCS) Snowfall Telemetry (SNOTEL) and snowcourse networks. Usually a single agency, but sometimes a consortium of interested parties, will jointly support a particular weather/climate network.

1.1.2. NPS I&M Networks

Within the NPS, the system for monitoring various attributes in the participating park units (about 270–280 in total) is divided into 32 NPS I&M networks. These networks are collections of park units grouped together around a common theme, typically geographical.

1.2. Weather versus Climate Definitions

It is also important to distinguish whether the primary use of a given station is for weather purposes or for climate purposes. Weather station networks are intended for near-real-time usage, where the precise circumstances of a set of measurements are typically less important. In these cases, changes in exposure or other attributes over time are not as critical. Climate networks, however, are intended for long-term tracking of atmospheric conditions. Siting and exposure are critical factors for climate networks, and it is vitally important that the observational circumstances remain essentially unchanged over the duration of the station record.

Figure 1.1. Map of the Chihuahuan Desert Network.

Some climate networks can be considered hybrids of weather/climate networks. These hybrid climate networks can supply information on a short-term "weather" time scale and a longer-term "climate" time scale.

In this report, "weather" generally refers to current (or near-real-time) atmospheric conditions, while "climate" is defined as the complete ensemble of statistical descriptors for temporal and spatial properties of atmospheric behavior (see Appendix A). Climate and weather phenomena shade gradually into each other and are ultimately inseparable.

1.3. Purpose of Measurements

Climate inventory and monitoring climate activities should be based on a set of guiding fundamental principles. Any evaluation of weather/climate monitoring programs begins with asking the following question:

- What is the purpose of weather and climate measurements?

Evaluation of past, present, or planned weather/climate monitoring activities must be based on the answer to this question.

Weather and climate data and information constitute a prominent and widely requested component of the NPS I&M networks (I&M 2006). Within the context of the NPS, the following services constitute the main purposes for recording weather and climate observations:

- Provide measurements for real-time operational needs and early warnings of potential hazards (landslides, mudflows, washouts, fallen trees, plowing activities, fire conditions, aircraft and watercraft conditions, road conditions, rescue conditions, fog, restoration and remediation activities, etc.).
- Provide visitor education and aid interpretation of expected and actual conditions for visitors while they are in the park and for deciding if and when to visit the park.
- Establish engineering and design criteria for structures, roads, culverts, etc., for human comfort, safety, and economic needs.
- Consistently monitor climate over the long-term to detect changes in environmental drivers affecting ecosystems, including both gradual and sudden events.
- Provide retrospective data to understand *a posteriori* changes in flora and fauna.
- Document for posterity the physical conditions in and near the park units, including mean, extreme, and variable measurements (in time and space) for all applications.

The last three items in the preceding list are pertinent primarily to the NPS I&M networks; however, all items are important to NPS operations and management. Most of the needs in this list overlap heavily. It is often impractical to operate separate climate measuring systems that also cannot be used to meet ordinary weather needs, where there is greater emphasis on timeliness and reliability.

1.4. Design of Climate-Monitoring Programs

Determining the purposes for collecting measurements in a given weather/climate monitoring program will guide the process of identifying weather/climate stations suitable for the monitoring program. The context for making these decisions is provided in Chapter 2 where background on the CHDN climate is presented. However, this process is only one step in evaluating and designing a climate-monitoring program. The following steps must also be included:

- Define park and network-specific monitoring needs and objectives.
- Identify locations and data repositories of existing and historic stations.
- Acquire existing data when necessary or practical.
- Evaluate the quality of existing data.
- Evaluate the adequacy of coverage of existing stations.
- Develop a protocol for monitoring the weather and climate, including the following:
  o Standardized summaries and reports of weather/climate data.
  o Data management (quality assurance and quality control, archiving, data access, etc.).
- Develop and implement a plan for installing or modifying stations, as necessary.

Throughout the design process, there are various factors that require consideration in evaluating weather and climate measurements. Many of these factors have been summarized by Dr. Tom Karl, director of the NOAA National Climatic Data Center (NCDC), and widely distributed as the "Ten Principles for Climate Monitoring" (Karl et al. 1996; NRC 2001). These principles are presented in Appendix B, and the guidelines are embodied in many of the comments made throughout this report. The most critical factors are presented here. In addition, an overview of requirements necessary to operate a climate network is provided in Appendix C, with further discussion in Appendix D.

1.4.1. Need for Consistency
A principal goal in climate monitoring is to detect and characterize slow and sudden changes in climate through time. This is of less concern for day-to-day weather changes, but it is of paramount importance for climate variability and change. There are many ways whereby changes in techniques for making measurements, changes in instruments or their exposures, or seemingly innocuous changes in site characteristics can lead to apparent changes in climate. Safeguards must be in place to avoid these false sources of temporal "climate" variability if we are to draw correct inferences about climate behavior over time from archived measurements.

For climate monitoring, consistency through time is vital, counting at least as important as absolute accuracy. Sensors record only what is occurring at the sensor—this is all they can detect. It is the responsibility of station or station network managers to ensure that observations are representative of the spatial and temporal climate scales that we wish to record.

1.4.2. Metadata
Changes in instruments, site characteristics, and observing methodologies can lead to apparent changes in climate through time. It is therefore vital to document all factors that can bear on the interpretation of climate measurements and to update the information repeatedly through time. This information ("metadata," data about data) has its own history and set of quality-control issues that parallel those of the actual data. There is no single standard for the content of climate metadata, but a simple rule suffices:

- Observers should record all information that could be needed in the future to interpret observations correctly without benefit of the observers' personal recollections.

Such documentation includes notes, drawings, site forms, and photos, which can be of inestimable value if taken in the correct manner. That stated, it is not always clear to the metadata provider *what is important* for posterity and *what will be important* in the future. It is almost impossible to "over document" a station. Station documentation is greatly underappreciated and is seldom thorough enough (especially for climate purposes). Insufficient attention to this issue often lowers the present and especially future value of otherwise useful data.

The convention followed throughout climatology is to refer to metadata as information about the measurement process, station circumstances, and data. The term "data" is reserved solely for the actual weather and climate records obtained from sensors.

1.4.3. Maintenance
Inattention to maintenance is the greatest source of failure in weather/climate stations and networks. Problems begin to occur soon after sites are deployed. A regular visit schedule must be implemented, where sites, settings (e.g., vegetation), sensors, communications, and data flow are checked routinely (once or twice a year at a minimum) and updated as necessary. Parts must be changed out for periodic recalibration or replacement. With adequate maintenance, the entire instrument suite should be replaced or completely refurbished about once every five to seven years.

Simple preventive maintenance is effective but requires much planning and skilled technical staff. Changes in technology and products require retraining and continual re-education. Travel, logistics, scheduling, and seasonal access restrictions consume major amounts of time and budget but are absolutely necessary. Without such attention, data gradually become less credible and then often are misused or not used at all.

1.4.4. Automated versus Manual Stations
Historic stations often have depended on manual observations and many continue to operate in this mode. Manual observations frequently produce excellent data sets. Sensors and data are simple and intuitive, well tested, and relatively cheap. Manual stations have much to offer in certain circumstances and can be a source of both primary and backup data. However, methodical consistency for manual measurements is a constant challenge, especially with a mobile work force. Operating manual stations takes time and needs to be done on a regular schedule, though sometimes the routine is welcome.

Nearly all newer stations are automated. Automated stations provide better time resolution, increased (though imperfect) reliability, greater capacity for data storage, and improved accessibility to large amounts of data. The purchase cost for automated stations is higher than for manual stations. A common expectation and serious misconception is that an automated station can be deployed and left to operate on its own. In reality, automation does not eliminate the need for people but rather changes the type of person that is needed. Skilled technical personnel are needed and must be readily available, especially if live communications exist and data gaps are not wanted. Site visits are needed at least annually and spare parts must be maintained. Typical annual costs for sensors and maintenance at the major national networks are $1500–2500 per station per year but these costs still can vary greatly depending on the kind of automated site.

1.4.5. Communications

With manual stations, the observer is responsible for recording and transmitting station data. Data from automated stations, however, can be transmitted quickly for access by research and operations personnel, which is a highly preferable situation. A comparison of communication systems for automated and manual stations shows that automated stations generally require additional equipment, more power, higher transmission costs, attention to sources of disruption or garbling, and backup procedures (e.g. manual downloads from data loggers).

Automated stations are capable of functioning normally without communication and retaining many months of data. At such sites, however, alerts about station problems are not possible, large gaps can accrue when accessible stations quit, and the constituencies needed to support such stations are smaller and less vocal. Two-way communications permit full recovery from disruptions, ability to reprogram data loggers remotely, and better opportunities for diagnostics and troubleshooting. In virtually all cases, two-way communications are much preferred to all other communication methods. However, two-way communications require considerations of cost, signal access, transmission rates, interference, and methods for keeping sensor and communication power loops separate. Two-way communications are frequently impossible (no service) or impractical, expensive, or power consumptive. Two-way methods (cellular, land line, radio, Internet) require smaller up-front costs as compared to other methods of communication and have variable recurrent costs, starting at zero. Satellite links work everywhere (except when blocked by trees or cliffs) and are quite reliable but are one-way and relatively slow, allow no re-transmissions, and require high up-front costs ($3000–4000) but no recurrent costs. Communications technology is changing constantly and requires vigilant attention by maintenance personnel.

1.4.6. Quality Assurance and Quality Control

Quality control and quality assurance are issues at every step through the entire sequence of sensing, communication, storage, retrieval, and display of environmental data. Quality assurance is an umbrella concept that covers all data collection and processing (start-to-finish) and ensures that credible information is available to the end user. Quality control has a more limited scope and is defined by the International Standards Organization as "the operational techniques and activities that are used to satisfy quality requirements." The central problem can be better appreciated if we approach quality control in the following way.

- Quality control is the evaluation, assessment, and rehabilitation of imperfect data by utilizing other imperfect data.

The quality of the data only decreases with time once the observation is made. The best and most effective quality control, therefore, consists in making high-quality measurements from the start and then successfully transmitting the measurements to an ingest process and storage site. Once the data are received from a monitoring station, a series of checks with increasing complexity can be applied, ranging from single-element checks (self-consistency) to multiple-element checks (inter-sensor consistency) to multiple-station/single-element checks (inter-station consistency). Suitable ancillary data (battery voltages, data ranges for all measurements, etc.) can prove extremely useful in diagnosing problems.

There is rarely a single technique in quality control procedures that will work satisfactorily for all situations. Quality-control procedures must be tailored to individual station circumstances, data access and storage methods, and climate regimes.

The fundamental issue in quality control centers on the tradeoff between falsely rejecting good data (Type I error) and falsely accepting bad data (Type II error). We cannot reduce the incidence of one type of error without increasing the incidence of the other type. In weather and climate data assessments, since good data are absolutely crucial for interpreting climate records properly, Type I errors are deemed far less desirable than Type II errors.

Not all observations are equal in importance. Quality-control procedures are likely to have the greatest difficulty evaluating the most extreme observations, where independent information usually must be sought and incorporated. Quality-control procedures involving more than one station usually involve a great deal of infrastructure with its own (imperfect) error-detection methods, which must be in place before a single value can be evaluated.

1.4.7. Standards

Although there is near-universal recognition of the value in systematic weather and climate measurements, these measurements will have little value unless they conform to accepted standards. There is not a single source for standards for collecting weather and climate data nor a single standard that meets all needs. Measurement standards have been developed by the World Meteorological Organization (WMO 1983; 2005), the American Association of State Climatologists (AASC 1985), the U.S. Environmental Protection Agency (EPA 1987), Finklin and Fischer (1990), the RAWS program (Bureau of Land Management [BLM] 1997), and the National Wildfire Coordinating Group (2004). Variations to these measurement standards also have been offered by instrument makers (e.g., Tanner 1990).

1.4.8. Who Makes the Measurements?

The lands under NPS stewardship provide many excellent locations to host the monitoring of climate by the NPS or other collaborators. These lands are largely protected from human development and other land changes that can impact observed climate records. Most park units historically have observed weather/climate elements as part of their overall mission. Many of these measurements come from station networks managed by other agencies, with observations taken or overseen by NPS personnel, in some cases, or by collaborators from the other agencies. National Park Service units that are small, lack sufficient resources, or lack sites presenting adequate exposure may benefit by utilizing weather/climate measurements collected from nearby stations.

2.0. Climate Background

Climate is a primary factor controlling the structure and function of ecosystems in the CHDN. An understanding of both current climate patterns and climate history in the CHDN is important to understanding and interpreting change and patterns in ecosystem attributes (Reiser et al. 2006). The modern distribution and ecology of plant and animal communities is linked to the climatic history of the CHDN region. This information provides significant power to the interpretation of other potential vital signs and provides a basis for understanding the response of desert ecosystems to future climate variation (Reiser et al. 2006). It is essential that the CHDN park units have an effective climate monitoring system to track climate changes and to aid in management decisions relating to these changes. In order to do this, it is essential to understand the climate characteristics of the CHDN, as discussed in this chapter.

2.1. Climate and the CHDN Environment

The climate within most of the CHDN is relatively uniform, with hot summers and cool to cold, dry winters (Schmidt 1979; Reiser et al. 2006). The CHDN is generally located at equal distances from the two primary moisture sources, the Gulf of Mexico and the Sea of Cortez. The CHDN sees little precipitation associated with mid-latitude storm events; much of its precipitation falls in the form of monsoonal rains during the summer months, especially in the Chihuahuan Desert ecoregion (Dinerstein et al. 2000; Ropelewski et al. 2005). The Tamaulipan Thornscrub, in eastern CHDN, generally receives more precipitation than the Chihuahuan Desert ecoregion. This precipitation is also more evenly distributed spatially than in the Chihuahuan Desert (Reiser et al. 2006).

Precipitation and solar radiation are two dominant inputs that drive the CHDN ecosystems. Seasonality, spatial variability, and duration of precipitation act to create pulses of water input in the CHDN (Snyder and Tartowski 2006). When combined with the effects of evaporation, these pulses have a strong influence on the distribution of soil resources that determine productivity and structure of other focal resources in CHDN ecosystems (Whitford 2002; Schlesinger et al. 2006). Solar radiation provides the initial energy that fuels primary production of vegetation and floral microbes in the minor aquatic systems and directly affects behavior and energy budgets of animals. Consequently, many plant and animal species have adapted special features to persist under conditions of low water availability and high solar radiation influx (Whitford 2002). Eolian (wind) processes can play a prominent role in the Chihuahuan Desert Ecosystem by affecting soil transport, redistribution of nutrients, and convection, which affects evaporation of soil moisture and plant desiccation (Gillette and Pitchford 2004; Okin et al. 2006). Large, rapid pulses of rainfall can cause flooding, disrupt normal hydrological cycles, and create temporary resources like playa lakes. Lightning can ignite community-changing fires. Over the long-term, climate driven processes interact with geologic materials and land forms to form or change desert soils (Monger and Bestelmeyer 2006).

Drought has been one of the principal historical sources of disturbance in the CHDN (Reiser et al. 2006). Drought is one of the principal factors limiting seedling establishment and productivity (Schulze et al. 1987; Osmond et al. 1987). This is done in part by impacting soil moisture gradients, which are a primary control on the distribution and vigor of plant communities (Pigott and Pigott 1993). Drought is also directly connected to wildfire frequency and intensity. For many years, wildfires have been an integral process in CHDN ecosystems. The extent to which fire occurred in southwestern grasslands varied geographically and was related to climatic variables such as seasonal and annual rainfall and physiographic variables such as elevation, slope, and aspect (Archer 1994). Fire may have been rare in desert grasslands and limited in extent, due to low biomass and a lack of continuity in fine fuels (Hastings and Turner 1965; York and Dick-Peddie 1969). In more mesic grassland and savanna systems where fire was a prevalent and recurring force, pre-historic frequency and intensity appear to have been regionally synchronized by climatic conditions (Swetnam and Betancourt 1990).

Prolonged drought, along with other disturbance agents such as excessive rainfall, and extreme temperatures can change structure and composition of focal resources. Extended dry periods, particularly when coupled with hot dry winds, can cause mass mortality of perennial grasses. This creates more and larger bare patches that are vulnerable to erosion. At some northern Chihuahuan Desert sites, prolonged drought during the 1950s has had a lasting effect on regeneration of black grama grasslands (Peters et al. 2006). Prolonged or rapid rainfall that cannot be absorbed by the soil can result in flooding that redistributes resources throughout the Desert Ecosystem and recharges aquifers and aquatic systems.

Climate change is an issue of much concern for the CHDN. Effects of future climate changes across the CHDN region may include increased surface temperatures; changes in the amount, seasonality, and distribution of precipitation; more frequent climatic extremes; and a greater variability in climate patterns (NAST 2001). Increasing atmospheric temperatures will accelerate the precipitation and evaporation components of the global hydrological budget, resulting in either a drier or wetter climate in central Texas in the future (Groeger and Bass 2005; Reiser et al. 2006). Such climate changes are widely predicted to increase the variability of weather events such as droughts and flood events.

Of all the possible impacts from climate change, global warming in particular is viewed as a likely future threat to the integrity of park ecosystems. Such changes may affect vegetation at the individual, population, or community level and precipitate changes in ecosystem function and structure (Weltzin and McPherson 1995). These factors will likely affect competitive interactions between plant and animal species currently coexisting under equilibrium conditions (Ehleringer et al. 1991). In the last 1-2 centuries, a rapid shift has occurred from areas dominated by desert grasslands to desert scrub vegetation across the CHDN; this shift is due in part to climate change (Dick-Peddie 1993). Potential management concerns included altered plant distribution and populations; reduced landscape connectivity, affecting the movement of animals and increasing local extinction events; changes to disease and insect outbreaks; and alterations to natural disturbance regimes (i.e., fire, flood). The greatest concern of CHDN staff is that dramatic changes in precipitation patterns will alter entire terrestrial, subterranean, and aquatic ecosystems.

However, the very high natural climate variability in the CHDN ecosystems may make the effects of climate change very hard to detect in the short run. In particular, precipitation in the Chihuahuan Desert is highly variable, due in part to the North American Monsoon System (NAMS) (Ropelewski et al. 2005). This variability in precipitation in desert locations, particularly during the monsoon season is also a constant impediment to biological research

(Reid and Reiser 2006). Investigators are repeatedly frustrated as they attempt to correlate biotic trend data with local climate. Precipitation measurements at one park or town location may have little to do with precipitation a few miles away. There is currently a lack of data that would permit analysis of this phenomenon.

2.2. Spatial Variability

The CHDN has more precipitation compared to other nearby desert ecoregions, with annual precipitation averaging somewhat above 200 mm across the network (Reid and Reiser 2006). In central and western portions of CHDN, topography plays a major role in defining the spatial distribution of precipitation (Figure 2.1). To the east, precipitation is inversely proportional to distance from the Gulf Coast, with an east-west gradient. Mean annual precipitation totals vary from well under 200 mm in lower elevations of western CHDN park units to around 500 mm in AMIS (see Reid and Reiser 2006).

Much of the precipitation in the CHDN is associated primarily with monsoon thunderstorm activity (Ropelewski et al. 2005). Western portions of the CHDN, including the Chihuahuan Desert ecoregion, are particularly susceptible to monsoon thunderstorm activity (Figure 2.2). Park units such as FODA and GUMO are known to receive well over 70 mm of precipitation on average during July (Reid and Reiser 2006) and higher elevations can receive over 100 mm of precipitation during this same period. The pattern of maximum precipitation occurring during the summer and fall months (see Figure 2.3) is common to all the park units except AMIS, which has more evenly distributed rainfall throughout the year (Schmidt 1979; 1990; 1995; Reid and Reiser 2006).

Mean annual temperatures across the CHDN vary largely as a function of elevation, increasing from the northwest to the southeast (Figure 2.4). The warmest park unit, annually, is AMIS, which has a mean annual temperature over 20°C (Reid and Reiser 2006). The coolest conditions are found in the higher elevations of GUMO, where mean annual temperatures are below 12°C in some locations. Temperatures are quite variable throughout the year in the CHDN. Winter temperatures, like annually-averaged temperatures, tend to follow a northwest-southeast gradient (e.g., Figure 2.5). Mean January temperatures range from below 4°C in WHSA to near 10°C in AMIS (Reid and Reiser 2006). January minimum temperatures in the CHDN are generally near or below freezing (0°C) except along the Rio Grande (Figure 2.5). July mean temperatures range from about 23°C at the GUMO visitor center to almost 30°C along the Rio Grande, including AMIS (Reid and Reiser 2006). Daytime maximum temperatures in July are coolest in FODA and the higher elevations of GUMO (under 30°C), while they are warmest along the Rio Grande, usually getting well above 30°C (Figure 2.6).

2.3. Temporal Variability

Interannual climate variations across the CHDN region are driven strongly by interannual variations in the intensity of NAMS (Douglas et al. 1993; Adams and Comrie 1997; Ropelewski et al. 2005). Variations in ENSO (El Niño Southern Oscillation) strongly influence interannual precipitation variations throughout the CHDN as well, with wetter conditions generally occurring during warm ENSO (El Niño) phases (Reiser et al. 2006). Little if any discernible trend can be noted in precipitation time series over the last century for the CHDN (Figure 2.7). However,

Figure 2.1. Mean annual precipitation, 1961-1990, for the CHDN.

12

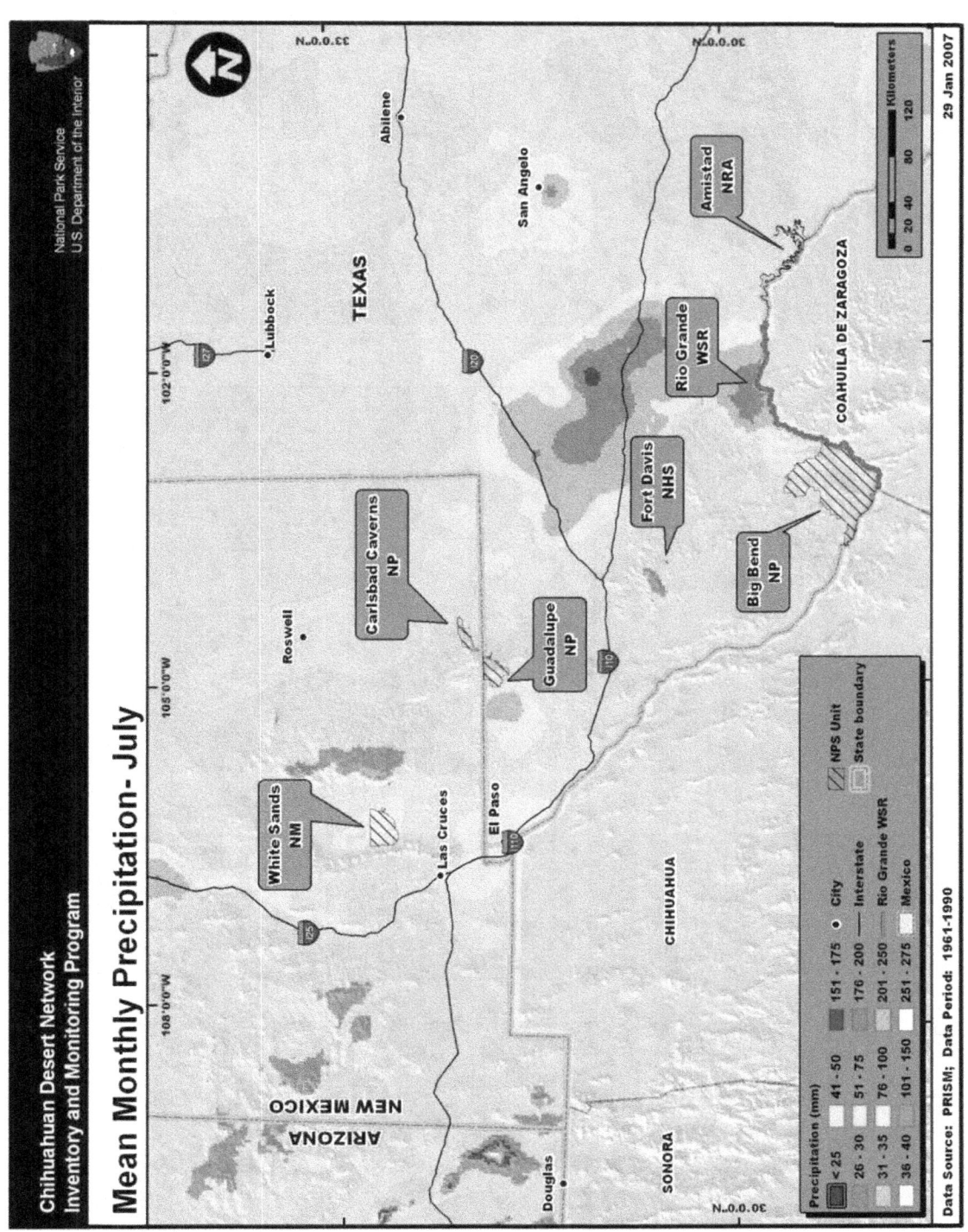

Figure 2.2. Mean July precipitation, 1961-1990, for the CHDN.

13

a)

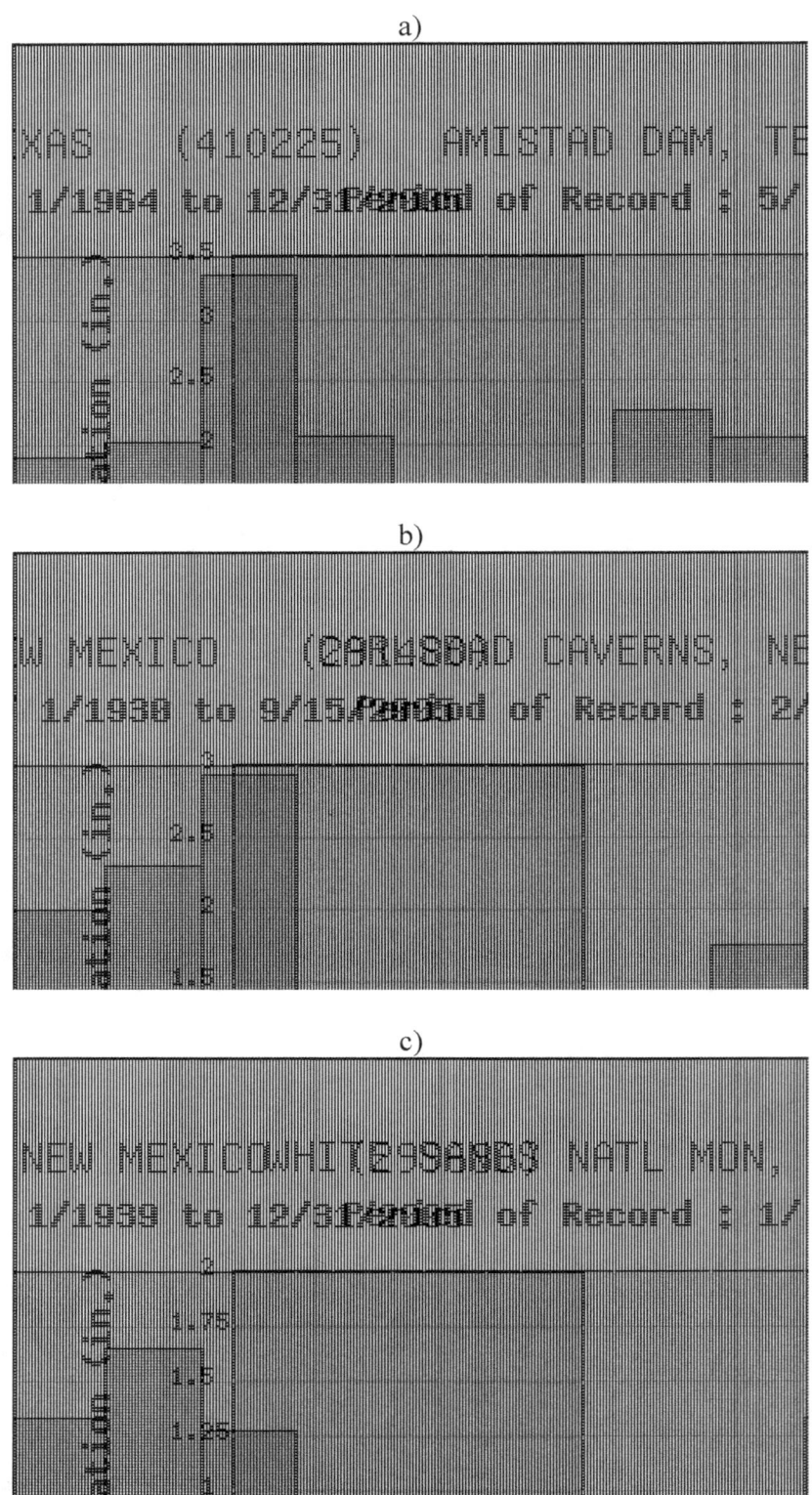

b)

c)

Figure 2.3. Mean monthly precipitation at selected locations in the CHDN. Locations include AMIS (a), CAVE (b), and WHSA (c).

Figure 2.4. Mean annual temperature, 1961-1990, for the CHDN.

15

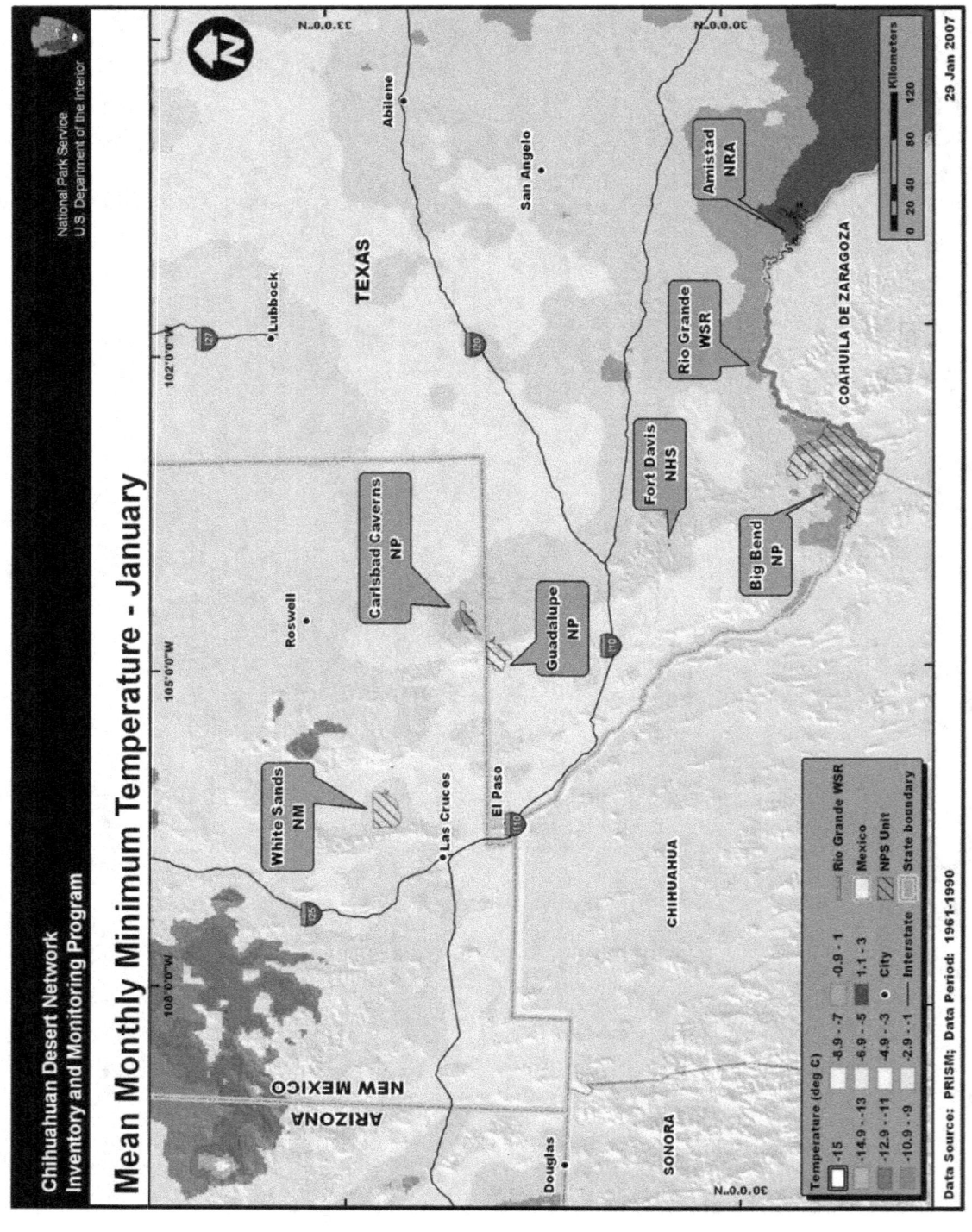

Figure 2.5. Mean January minimum temperature, 1961-1990, for the CHDN.

16

Figure 2.6. Mean July maximum temperature, 1961-1990, for the CHDN.

17

a)

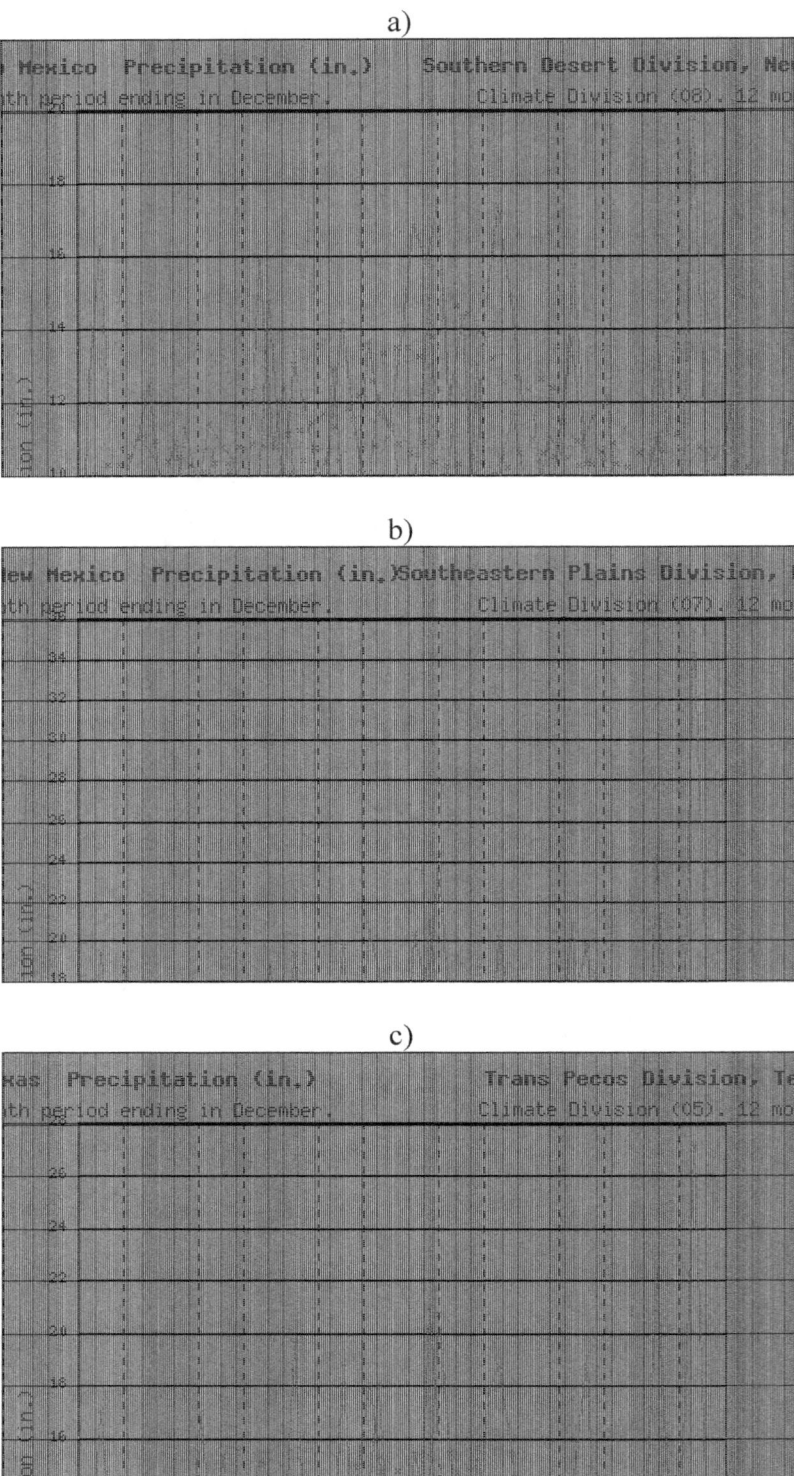

b)

c)

Figure 2.7. Precipitation time series, 1895-2005, for selected regions in the CHDN. These include twelve-month precipitation (ending in December) (red), 10-year running mean (blue), mean (green), and plus/minus one standard deviation (green dotted). Locations include southwestern New Mexico (a), southeastern New Mexico (b), and western Texas (c).

there are notable dry and wet periods. The 1950s stand out as being particularly dry across the CHDN. Conditions gradually became wetter through the 1980s, while somewhat drier conditions have been the rule from the 1990s through present. A very wet year for the entire CHDN region occurred in 1941. While annual precipitation across CHDN park units generally ranges between 100-500 mm, precipitation totals for 1941 included almost 1100 mm for CAVE (1098 mm) and GUMO (1079 mm at Pine Springs). Even WHSA recorded over 500 mm of precipitation that year. Trends in temperatures across the CHDN (Figure 2.8) are difficult to detect. It is generally apparent, however, that temperatures have become warmer over the past 2-3 decades. It is not clear how much of this observed pattern may be due to discontinuities in temperature records at individual stations, caused by artificial changes such as station moves. These patterns highlight the emphasis on measurement consistency that is needed in order to properly detect long-term climatic changes.

2.4. Parameter Regression on Independent Slopes Model

The climate maps presented in this report were generated using the Parameter Regression on Independent Slopes Model (PRISM). This model was developed to address the extreme spatial and elevation gradients exhibited by the climate of the western U.S. (Daly et al. 1994; 2002; Gibson et al. 2002; Doggett et al. 2004). The maps produced through PRISM have undergone rigorous evaluation in the western U.S. This model was originally developed to provide climate information at scales matching available land-cover maps to assist in ecologic modeling. The PRISM technique accounts for the scale-dependent effects of topography on mean values of climate elements. Elevation provides the first-order constraint for the mapped climate fields, with slope and orientation (aspect) providing second-order constraints. The model has been enhanced gradually to address inversions, coast/land gradients, and climate patterns in small-scale trapping basins. Monthly climate fields are generated by PRISM to account for seasonal variations in elevation gradients in climate elements. These monthly climate fields then can be combined into seasonal and annual climate fields. Since PRISM maps are grid maps, they do not replicate point values but rather, for a given grid cell, represent the grid-cell average of the climate variable in question at the average elevation for that cell. The model relies on observed surface and upper-air measurements to estimate spatial climate fields.

a)

b)

c)

Figure 2.8. Temperature time series, 1895-2005, for selected regions in the CHDN. These include twelve-month average temperature (ending in December) (red), 10-year running mean (blue), mean (green), and plus/minus one standard deviation (green dotted). Locations include southwestern New Mexico (a), southeastern New Mexico (b), and western Texas (c).

3.0. Methods

Having discussed the climatic characteristics of the CHDN, we now present the procedures that were used to obtain information for weather/climate stations within the CHDN. This information was obtained from various sources, as mentioned in the following paragraphs. Retrieval of station metadata constituted a major component of this work.

3.1. Metadata Retrieval

A key component of station inventories is determining the kinds of observations that have been conducted over time, by whom, and in what manner; when each type of observation began and ended; and whether these observations are still being conducted. Metadata about the observational process (Table 3.1) generally consist of a series of vignettes that apply to time intervals and, therefore, constitute a *history* rather than a single snapshot. An expanded list of relevant metadata fields for this inventory is provided in Appendix E. This report has relied on metadata records from three sources: (a) Western Regional Climate Center (WRCC), (b) NPS personnel, and (c) other knowledgeable personnel, such as state climate office staff.

The initial metadata sources for this report were stored at WRCC. This regional climate center (RCC) acts as a working repository of many western climate records, including the main networks outlined in this section. The WRCC conducts live and periodic data collection (ingests) from all major national and western weather/climate networks. These networks include the COOP network, the Surface Airways Observation network (SAO) operated by NWS and the Federal Aviation Administration (FAA), the interagency RAWS network, and various smaller networks. The WRCC is expanding its capability to ingest information from other networks as resources permit and usefulness dictates. This center has relied heavily on historic archives (in many cases supplemented with live ingests) to assess the quantity (not necessarily quality) of data available for NPS I&M network applications.

The primary source of metadata at WRCC is the Applied Climate Information System (ACIS), a joint effort among RCCs and other NOAA entities. Metadata for CHDN weather/climate stations identified from the ACIS database are available in file "CHDN_from_ACIS.tar.gz" (see Appendix F). Historic metadata pertaining to major climate- and weather-observing systems in the U.S. are stored in ACIS where metadata are linked to the observed data. A distributed system, ACIS is synchronized among the RCCs. Mainstream software is utilized, including Postgress, Python™, and Java™ programming languages; CORBA®-compliant network software; and industry-standard, nonproprietary hardware and software. Metadata and data for all major national climate and weather networks have been entered into the ACIS database. For this project, the available metadata from many smaller networks also have been entered but in most cases the actual data have not yet been entered. Data sets are in the NetCDF (Network Common Data Form) format, but the design allows for integration with legacy systems, including non-NetCDF files (used at WRCC) and additional metadata (added for this project). The ACIS also supports a suite of products to visualize or summarize data from these data sets. National climate-monitoring maps are updated daily using the ACIS data feed. The developmental phases of ACIS have utilized metadata supplied by the NCDC and NWS with many tens of thousands of entries, screened as well as possible for duplications, mistakes, and omissions.

Table 3.1. Primary metadata fields for CHDN weather/climate stations. Explanations are provided as appropriate.

Metadata Field	Notes
Station name	Station name associated with network listed in "Climate Network."
Latitude	Numerical value (units: see coordinate units).
Longitude	Numerical value (units: see coordinate units).
Coordinate units	Latitude/longitude (units: decimal degrees, degree-minute-second, etc.).
Datum	Datum used as basis for coordinates: WGS 84, NAD 83, etc.
Elevation	Elevation of station above mean sea level (m).
Slope	Slope of ground surface below station (degrees).
Aspect	Azimuth that ground surface below station faces.
Climate division	NOAA climate division where station is located. Climate divisions are NOAA-specified zones sharing similar climate and hydrology characteristics.
Country	Country where station is located.
State	State where station is located.
County	County where station is located.
Weather/climate network	Primary weather/climate network the station belongs to (COOP, RAWS, etc.).
NPS unit code	Four-letter code identifying park unit where station resides.
NPS unit name	Full name of park unit.
NPS unit type	National park, national monument, etc.
UTM zone	If UTM is the only coordinate system available.
Location notes	Useful information not already included in "station narrative."
Climate variables	Temperature, precipitation, etc.
Installation date	Date of station installation.
Removal date	Date of station removal.
Station photograph	Digital image of station.
Photograph date	Date photograph was taken.
Photographer	Name of person who took the photograph.
Station narrative	Anything related to general site description; may include site exposure, characteristics of surrounding vegetation, driving directions, etc.
Contact name	Name of the person involved with station operation.
Organization	Group or agency affiliation of contact person.
Contact type	Designation that identifies contact person as the station owner, observer, maintenance person, data manager, etc.
Position/job title	Official position/job title of contact person.
Address	Address of contact person.
E-mail address	E-mail address of contact person.
Phone	Phone number of contact person (and extension if available).
Contact notes	Other information needed to reach contact person.

Two types of information have been used to complete the CHDN climate station inventory.

- Station inventories: Information about observational procedures, latitude/longitude, elevation, measured elements, measurement frequency, sensor types, exposures, ground cover and vegetation, data-processing details, network, purpose, and managing individual or agency, etc.

- Data inventories: Information about measured data values including completeness, seasonality, data gaps, representation of missing data, flagging systems, how special circumstances in the data record are denoted, etc.

This is not a straightforward process. Extensive searches are typically required to develop historic station and data inventories. Both types of inventories frequently contain information gaps and often rely on tacit and unrealistic assumptions. Sources of information for these inventories frequently are difficult to recover or are undocumented and unreliable. In many cases, the actual weather/climate data available from different sources are not linked directly to metadata records. To the extent that actual data can be acquired (rather than just metadata), it is possible to cross-check these records and perform additional assessments based on the amount and completeness of the data.

Certain types of weather/climate networks that possess any of the following attributes have not been considered for inclusion in the inventory:

- Private networks with proprietary access and/or inability to obtain or provide sufficient metadata.
- Private weather enthusiasts (often with high-quality data) whose metadata are not available and whose data are not readily accessible.
- Unofficial observers supplying data to the NWS (lack of access to current data and historic archives; lack of metadata).
- Networks having no available historic data.
- Networks having poor-quality metadata.
- Networks having poor access to metadata.
- Real-time networks having poor access to real-time data.

Previous inventory efforts at WRCC have shown that for the weather networks identified in the preceding list, in light of the need for quality data to track weather and climate, the resources required and difficulty encountered in obtaining metadata or data are prohibitively large.

3.2. Criteria for Locating Stations
To identify weather and climate stations for each park unit in the CHDN we selected only those stations located within a specified buffer distance of the CHDN park units. This buffer distance was 50 km for all CHDN park units except BIBE, GUMO, and RIGR, which used 100-km buffer distances. These buffer distances were selected in an attempt to include at least a few automated stations from major networks such as SAO.

The station locator maps presented in Chapter 4 were designed to show clearly the spatial distributions of all major weather/climate station networks in CHDN. We recognize that other mapping formats may be more suitable for other specific needs.

4.0. Station Inventory

An objective of this report is to show the locations of weather/climate stations for the CHDN region in relation to the boundaries of the NPS park units within the CHDN. A station does not have to be within park boundaries to provide useful data and information for a park unit.

4.1. Climate and Weather Networks

Most stations in the CHDN region are associated with at least one of nine major weather/climate networks (Table 4.1). Brief descriptions of each weather/climate network are provided below (see Appendix G for greater detail).

Table 4.1. Weather/climate networks represented within the CHDN.

Acronym	Name
CASTNet	Clean Air Status and Trends Network
COOP	NWS Cooperative Observer Program
CWOP	Citizen Weather Observer Program
GPMP	NPS Gaseous Pollutant Monitoring Program
GPS-MET	NOAA ground-based GPS meteorology network
NADP	National Atmospheric Deposition Program
RAWS	Remote Automated Weather Station network
SAO	NWS/FAA Surface Airways Observation network
WX4U	Weather For You network

4.1.1. Clean Air Status and Trends Network (CASTNet)

CASTNet is primarily an air-quality monitoring network managed by the EPA. Standard hourly weather and climate elements are measured and include temperature, wind, humidity, solar radiation, soil temperature, and sometimes moisture. These elements are intended to support interpretation of air-quality parameters that also are measured at CASTNet sites. Data records at CASTNet sites are generally one–two decades in length.

4.1.2. NWS Cooperative Observer Program (COOP)

The COOP network has been a foundation of the U.S. climate program for decades and continues to play an important role. Manual measurements are made by volunteers and consist of daily maximum and minimum temperatures, observation-time temperature, daily precipitation, daily snowfall, and snow depth. When blended with NWS measurements, the data set is known as SOD, or "Summary of the Day." The quality of data from COOP sites ranges from excellent to modest.

4.1.3. Citizen Weather Observer Program (CWOP)

The CWOP network consists primarily of automated weather stations operated by private citizens who have either an Internet connection and/or a wireless Ham radio setup. Data from CWOP stations are specifically intended for use in research, education, and homeland security activities. Although standard meteorological elements such as temperature, precipitation, and wind are measured at all CWOP stations, station characteristics do vary, including sensor types and site exposure.

4.1.4. Gaseous Pollutant Monitoring Program (GPMP)
The GPMP network measures hourly meteorological data in support of pollutant monitoring activities. Measured elements include temperature, precipitation, humidity, wind, and solar radiation. These data are generally of high quality, with records up to two decades in length.

4.1.5. NOAA Ground-Based GPS Meteorology (GPS-MET)
The GPS-MET network is the first network of its kind dedicated to GPS (Global Positioning System) meteorology (see Duan et al. 1996), which utilizes the radio signals broadcast by the satellite for atmospheric remote sensing. GPS meteorology applications have evolved along two paths: ground-based (Bevis et al. 1992) and space-based (Yuan et al. 1993). For more information, please see Appendix G. The stations identified in this inventory are all ground-based. The GPS-MET network was developed in response to the need for improved moisture observations to support weather forecasting, climate monitoring, and other research activities. The primary goals of this network are to measure atmospheric water vapor using ground-based GPS receivers, facilitate the operational use of these data, and encourage usage of GPS meteorology for atmospheric research and other applications. GPS-MET is a collaboration between NOAA and several other governmental and university organizations and institutions. Ancillary meteorological observations at GPS-MET stations include temperature, relative humidity, and pressure.

4.1.6. National Atmospheric Deposition Program (NADP)
The purpose of the NADP network is to monitor primarily wet deposition at selected sites around the U.S. and its territories. The network is a collaborative effort among several agencies including USDA and the U.S. Geological Survey (USGS). This network also includes sites with the Mercury Deposition Network (MDN). Precipitation is the primary climate parameter measured at NADP sites.

4.1.7. Remote Automated Weather Station Network (RAWS)
The RAWS network is administered through many land management agencies, particularly the BLM and the Forest Service. Hourly meteorology elements are measured and include temperature, wind, humidity, solar radiation, barometric pressure, fuel temperature, and precipitation (when temperatures are above freezing). The fire community is the primary client for RAWS data. These sites are remote and data typically are transmitted via GOES (Geostationary Operational Environmental Satellite). Some sites operate all winter. Most data records for RAWS sites began during or after the mid-1980s.

4.1.8. NWS/FAA Surface Airways Observation Network (SAO)
These stations are located usually at major airports and military bases. Almost all SAO sites are automated. The hourly data measured at these sites include temperature, precipitation, humidity, wind, pressure, sky cover, ceiling, visibility, and current weather. Most data records begin during or after the 1940s, and these data are generally of high quality.

4.1.9. Weather For You Network (WX4U)
The WX4U network is a nationwide collection of weather stations run by local observers. Data quality varies with site. Standard meteorological elements are measured and usually include temperature, precipitation, wind, and humidity.

4.1.10. Weather Bureau Army Navy (WBAN)
Some stations are identified in this report as WBAN stations. This is a station identification system rather than a true weather/climate network. Stations identified with WBAN are largely historical stations that reported meteorological observations on the WBAN weather observation forms that were common during the early and middle parts of the twentieth century. The use of WBAN numbers to identify stations was one of the first attempts in the U.S. to use a coordinated station numbering scheme between several weather station networks, such as the COOP and SAO networks.

4.1.11. Other Networks
In addition to the major networks mentioned above, there are various networks that are operated for specific purposes by specific organizations or governmental agencies or scientific research projects. These networks could be present within CHDN but have not been identified in this report. Some of the commonly used networks include the following:

- NOAA upper-air stations
- Federal and state departments of transportation
- U.S. Department of Energy Surface Radiation Budget Network (Surfrad)
- Park-specific-monitoring networks and stations
- Other research or project networks having many possible owners

4.2. Station Locations
The major weather/climate networks in the CHDN (discussed in Section 4.1) have at most several stations at or inside each park unit (Table 4.2). Most of these stations are COOP stations.

Table 4.2. Number of stations within or nearby CHDN park units. Numbers are listed by park unit and by weather/climate network. Figures in parentheses indicate the numbers of stations within park boundaries.

Network	AMIS	BIBE	CAVE	FODA	GUMO	RIGR	WHSA
CASTNet	0(0)	1(1)	0(0)	0(0)	0(0)	1(0)	0(0)
COOP	30(2)	25(8)	25(1)	25(0)	22(0)	57(0)	16(1)
CWOP	0(0)	3(0)	0(0)	5(0)	0(0)	0(0)	2(0)
GPMP	0(0)	1(1)	1(0)	0(0)	1(0)	1(0)	0(0)
GPS-MET	0(0)	0(0)	0(0)	0(0)	0(0)	0(0)	1(0)
NADP	0(0)	1(1)	1(0)	0(0)	1(1)	1(0)	1(0)
RAWS	0(0)	2(2)	5(1)	2(0)	5(2)	2(0)	7(0)
SAO	2(0)	0(0)	2(0)	3(0)	2(0)	3(0)	5(0)
WX4U	0(0)	1(0)	0(0)	1(0)	0(0)	0(0)	0(0)
Other	1(0)	0(0)	1(0)	3(0)	1(0)	1(0)	10(0)
Total	33(2)	34(13)	35(2)	39(0)	32(3)	66(0)	42(1)

Lists of stations have been compiled for the CHDN. It is worth noting again that a station does not have to be within the boundaries to provide useful data and information regarding the park unit in question. Some might be physically *within* the administrative or political boundaries, whereas others might be just outside, or even some distance away, but would be *nearby* in behavior and representativeness. What constitutes "useful" and "representative" are also significant questions, whose answers can vary according to application, type of element, period of record, procedural or methodological observation conventions, and the like.

Besides the stations listed here, the weather instrumentation at Indio Mountain Research Station (http://www.utep.edu/indio/), located near Van Horn, Texas, provides useful weather data for the region. This facility is located about 100 km south of GUMO and 100 km northwest of FODA. In addition, the Jornada Basin Long Term Ecological Research (LTER) site (http://www.lternet.edu/sites/jrn/), about 25 km west of WHSA, has operated an automated weather station since 1985, about km west of WHSA. At the time of this report, data access could not be verified for these stations so they are not listed within the following station tables.

4.2.1. New Mexico and extreme West Texas

The two stations identified within the boundaries of CAVE are currently active (Table 4.3). Both of these are located near the main visitor center for CAVE, in the eastern portion of the park (Figure 4.1). One of these active stations is a long-term COOP climate station that has been active since 1930 (Carlsbad Caverns), while the other station, a RAWS station (Batdraw) provides near-real-time weather data within the park unit. The COOP station "Carlsbad Caverns"

Table 4.3. Weather/climate stations for the CHDN park units in New Mexico and extreme West Texas. Stations inside park units and within a specified buffer distance of the park unit boundary (50 km for CAVE and WHSA, 100 km for GUMO) are included. Missing entries are indicated by "M".

Name	Lat.	Lon.	Elev. (m)	Network	Start	End	In Park?
Carlsbad Caverns National Park (CAVE)							
Carlsbad Caverns	32.177	-104.443	1342	COOP	2/1/1930	Present	Yes
Batdraw	32.179	-104.442	1311	RAWS	3/1/1997	Present	Yes
Brantley Dam	32.516	-104.383	979	COOP	8/1/1987	Present	No
Carlsbad	32.348	-104.223	951	COOP	2/1/1900	Present	No
Carlsbad	32.338	-104.263	985	COOP	1/1/1930	Present	No
Carlsbad 8 NW	32.517	-104.333	967	COOP	8/1/1978	12/1/1992	No
Carson Seep Near	32.100	-104.767	1891	COOP	7/1/1895	12/31/1938	No
Cienega 5 SSW	32.033	-105.100	1159	COOP	11/1/1955	4/1/1964	No
Dark Canyon Road	32.283	-104.516	1196	COOP	8/1/2005	Present	No
Eddy	32.367	-104.283	951	COOP	1/1/1897	9/30/1899	No
Gardner Ranch	32.200	-105.133	1341	COOP	7/1/1942	9/30/1943	No
Gowdy Ranch	32.317	-105.100	1220	COOP	3/1/1962	6/1/1967	No
Lake Avalon	32.483	-104.250	979	COOP	8/1/1914	2/11/1980	No
Lake McMillan	32.600	-104.333	1000	COOP	1/1/1940	2/28/1950	No
Lakewood	32.633	-104.383	1006	COOP	1/1/1912	5/31/1928	No
Loving	32.283	-104.083	921	COOP	11/1/1917	2/28/1950	No
Marathon Gas Plant	32.450	-104.533	1164	COOP	8/1/1978	12/1/1992	No
Orange	32.017	-105.150	1105	COOP	2/1/1906	9/30/1910	No
Pine Springs	31.890	-104.808	1704	COOP	12/1/1938	Present	No
Pine Springs	31.831	-104.809	1663	COOP	2/1/1931	Present	No
Queen	32.194	-104.740	1780	COOP	4/1/2000	9/19/2006	No
Queen R.S.	32.200	-104.733	1784	COOP	1/1/1963	4/30/1975	No

Name	Lat.	Lon.	Elev. (m)	Network	Start	End	In Park?
Salt Flat	31.750	-105.083	1133	COOP	1/1/1934	1/31/1958	No
Salt Flat	31.746	-105.081	1134	COOP	9/1/1978	7/1/1999	No
Salt Flat 10 ENE	31.783	-104.900	1186	COOP	12/1/1958	9/30/1978	No
Shattucks	32.250	-104.550	1829	COOP	1/1/1897	7/31/1900	No
Guadalupe Mountains	31.833	-104.809	1664	GPMP	8/1/1987	10/31/1992	No
Guad. Mtns. NP Frijole R.S.	31.908	-104.803	1734	NADP	6/5/1984	Present	No
Bandana Point	32.326	-104.558	1323	RAWS	3/1/1990	2/28/1997	No
Guadalupe Peak	31.925	-104.825	2364	RAWS	7/1/1985	Present	No
Pinery	31.894	-104.798	1640	RAWS	5/1/2001	Present	No
Queen	32.204	-104.690	1708	RAWS	12/1/2004	Present	No
Carlsbad	32.338	-104.263	985	SAO	1/1/1930	Present	No
Pine Springs	31.831	-104.809	1663	SAO	2/1/1931	Present	No
Carlsbad	32.350	-104.250	991	WBAN	9/1/1942	9/30/1945	No

Guadalupe Mountains National Park (GUMO)

Name	Lat.	Lon.	Elev. (m)	Network	Start	End	In Park?
Guad. Mtns. NP Frijole R.S.	31.908	-104.803	1734	NADP	6/5/1984	Present	Yes
Guadalupe Peak	31.925	-104.825	2364	RAWS	7/1/1985	Present	Yes
Pinery	31.894	-104.798	1640	RAWS	5/1/2001	Present	Yes
Brantley Dam	32.516	-104.383	979	COOP	8/1/1987	Present	No
Carlsbad	32.348	-104.223	951	COOP	2/1/1900	Present	No
Carlsbad	32.338	-104.263	985	COOP	1/1/1930	Present	No
Carlsbad Caverns	32.177	-104.443	1342	COOP	2/1/1930	Present	No
Carson Seep Near	32.100	-104.767	1891	COOP	7/1/1895	12/31/1938	No
Cienega 5 SSW	32.033	-105.100	1159	COOP	11/1/1955	4/1/1964	No
Cornudas Svc. Stn.	31.780	-105.470	1366	COOP	6/1/1940	Present	No
Dark Canyon Road	32.283	-104.516	1196	COOP	8/1/2005	Present	No
Dell City 5 SSW	31.877	-105.237	1149	COOP	4/1/1955	Present	No
Eddy	32.367	-104.283	951	COOP	1/1/1897	9/30/1899	No
Gardner Ranch	32.200	-105.133	1341	COOP	7/1/1942	9/30/1943	No
Gowdy Ranch	32.317	-105.100	1220	COOP	3/1/1962	6/1/1967	No
Marathon Gas Plant	32.450	-104.533	1164	COOP	8/1/1978	12/1/1992	No
Orange	32.017	-105.150	1105	COOP	2/1/1906	9/30/1910	No
Pine Springs	31.890	-104.808	1704	COOP	12/1/1938	Present	No
Pine Springs	31.831	-104.809	1663	COOP	2/1/1931	Present	No
Queen	32.194	-104.740	1780	COOP	4/1/2000	9/19/2006	No
Queen R.S.	32.200	-104.733	1784	COOP	1/1/1963	4/30/1975	No
Salt Flat	31.750	-105.083	1133	COOP	1/1/1934	1/31/1958	No
Salt Flat	31.746	-105.081	1134	COOP	9/1/1978	7/1/1999	No
Salt Flat 10 ENE	31.783	-104.900	1186	COOP	12/1/1958	9/30/1978	No
Shattucks	32.250	-104.550	1829	COOP	1/1/1897	7/31/1900	No
Guadalupe Mountains	31.833	-104.809	1664	GPMP	8/1/1987	10/31/1992	No
Bandana Point	32.326	-104.558	1323	RAWS	3/1/1990	2/28/1997	No
Batdraw	32.179	-104.442	1311	RAWS	3/1/1997	Present	No
Queen	32.204	-104.690	1708	RAWS	12/1/2004	Present	No
Carlsbad	32.338	-104.263	985	SAO	1/1/1930	Present	No
Pine Springs	31.831	-104.809	1663	SAO	2/1/1931	Present	No
Carlsbad	32.350	-104.250	991	WBAN	9/1/1942	9/30/1945	No

Name	Lat.	Lon.	Elev. (m)	Network	Start	End	In Park?
White Sands National Monument (WHSA)							
White Sands Natl. Mon.	32.782	-106.175	1218	COOP	1/1/1939	Present	Yes
Alamogordo	32.918	-105.947	1326	COOP	7/1/1909	Present	No
Alamogordo 1	32.867	-105.933	M	COOP	1/1/1892	3/31/1943	No
Alamogordo Filter Plant	32.967	-105.933	1440	COOP	11/1/1958	5/31/1968	No
Boyds Ranch	32.333	-106.583	1783	COOP	6/1/1914	3/31/1916	No
Cloud Country Club	32.967	-105.750	2693	COOP	7/1/1973	3/20/1979	No
Cloudcroft	32.967	-105.750	2689	COOP	12/1/1901	6/10/1987	No
Cloudcroft	32.954	-105.735	2640	COOP	6/11/1987	Present	No
Cloudcroft 2	32.950	-105.733	2654	COOP	5/1/1948	5/31/1959	No
Escondido	32.600	-106.017	1223	COOP	7/1/1909	8/31/1914	No
Jornada Exp. Range	32.617	-106.741	1300	COOP	6/1/1914	Present	No
Mountain Park	32.955	-105.824	2067	COOP	10/15/1894	Present	No
Orogrande	32.379	-106.091	1275	COOP	12/1/1904	Present	No
Sacramento Canyon	32.683	-105.717	2257	COOP	10/1/1949	3/31/1954	No
Timberon	32.643	-105.693	2137	COOP	5/28/1998	2/11/2004	No
Tularosa	33.072	-106.042	1350	COOP	5/1/1906	Present	No
BENRDG Benson Ridge	32.874	-105.774	2995	CWOP	M	Present	No
CW5738 High Rolls	32.940	-105.842	2100	CWOP	M	Present	No
White Sands	32.410	-106.350	1226	GPS-MET	M	Present	No
Mayhill	32.909	-105.471	2009	NADP	1/24/1984	Present	No
Bosque	32.800	-106.883	1372	RAWS	3/1/1992	Present	No
Cosmic	32.779	-105.819	2774	RAWS	6/1/1990	Present	No
Dripping Springs	32.323	-106.587	1881	RAWS	2/1/1994	Present	No
Mayhill	32.983	-105.500	2042	RAWS	12/1/1985	Present	No
Mescal	33.167	-105.833	1898	RAWS	9/1/2000	Present	No
Organ Mountains	32.410	-106.550	1558	RAWS	5/1/1985	8/31/1993	No
San Andres	32.580	-106.525	1871	RAWS	7/1/1997	Present	No
Alamogordo	32.833	-106.000	1279	SAO	11/1/1959	6/23/1989	No
Cloudcroft	32.954	-105.735	2640	SAO	6/11/1987	Present	No
Holloman	32.850	-106.100	1267	SAO	9/1/1942	Present	No
Las Cruces	32.383	-106.483	1292	SAO	11/1/1946	Present	No
Northrup	32.900	-106.400	1189	SAO	1/1/1989	Present	No
Frye Site	32.500	-106.417	1270	WBAN	1/1/1960	1/31/1961	No
Holloman AFB	32.850	-106.083	1251	WBAN	1/1/1989	Present	No
Jallen Site	33.183	-106.483	1236	WBAN	1/1/1956	1/31/1961	No
Oro Grande	32.400	-106.150	1262	WBAN	5/1/1946	4/30/1948	No
Sacramento AFS	32.800	-105.817	2811	WBAN	6/1/1948	7/31/1948	No
White Sands	32.883	-106.350	1227	WBAN	4/1/1963	Present	No
White Sands	32.367	-106.400	1196	WBAN	12/22/1979	Present	No
White Sands	32.633	-106.400	1204	WBAN	M	Present	No
White Sands Miss. Rng.	32.350	-106.367	1224	WBAN	1/1/1989	Present	No
White Sands Up. Rng.	33.217	-106.450	1244	WBAN	4/1/1948	4/30/1948	No

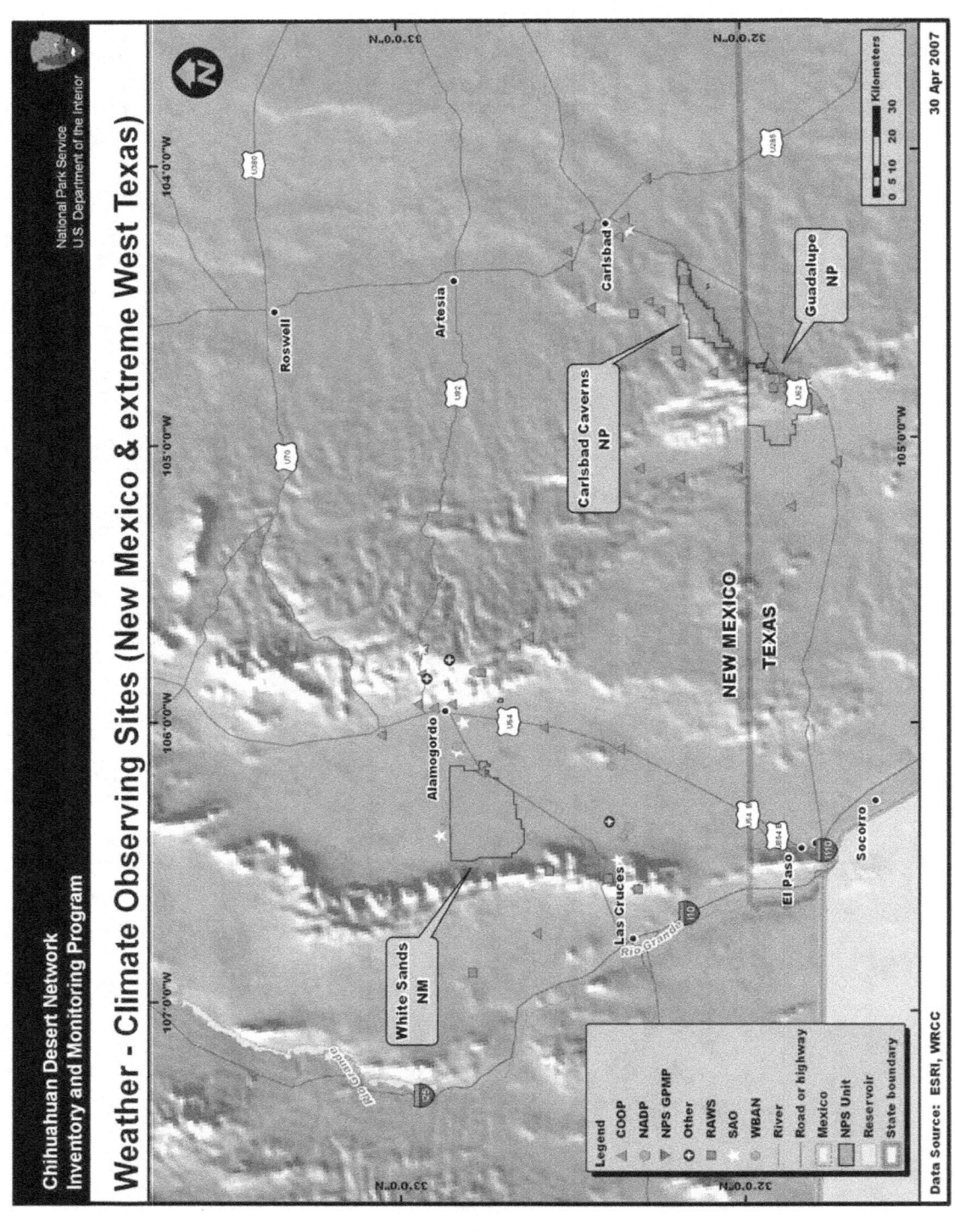

Figure 4.1. Station locations for the CHDN park units in New Mexico and extreme West Texas.

has taken measurements since 1930. The data record at this station is quite complete, although it has become more incomplete during the past 1-2 years.

Four active COOP stations were identified within 50 km of the boundaries of CAVE. The closest COOP station outside of CAVE is "Dark Canyon Road," which has been operating since August 2005. This station is 10 km northwest of CAVE (Figure 4.1). The longest data record comes from the COOP station "Carlsbad," which is 22 km northeast of CAVE and has been taking measurements since 1900 (Table 4.3). The record at this site is very complete from 1990 onward. Scattered data gaps occur elsewhere in the record for "Carlsbad," including no weekend observations during the 1970s and early 1980s. The COOP station "Pine Springs," located 26 km southwest of CAVE, also provides a long-term record for CAVE, going back to 1931. However, the reliability of the data record at this site is questionable until 1987.

The primary sources of near-real-time weather data outside of CAVE are the SAO stations at Carlsbad and Pine Springs and three RAWS stations located south and west of CAVE (Figure 4.1; Table 4.3). Both of the SAO stations have data records going back to the 1930s. The longest RAWS record comes from the station "Guadalupe Peak," located 19 km southwest of CAVE in GUMO. This RAWS station has been active since 1985 and has had a fairly complete data record with the exception of a few data gaps in the late 1980s and early 1990s. The latest gap occurred from October 1992 to February 1993.

Three stations were identified within the boundaries of GUMO, all of which are still active (Table 4.3). These stations are associated with the NADP and RAWS networks, and are concentrated primarily in eastern GUMO (Figure 4.1). The longest data record comes from the NADP station "Guadalupe Mtns. NP Frijole R.S." (1984-present).

No long-term climate records were identified within GUMO. The COOP station "Pine Springs" is located just 1 km from GUMO and is the closest long-term climate record. However, as discussed previously, the reliability of this record is in question before 1987. The COOP station "Carlsbad Caverns" is 34 km northeast of GUMO and provides a more reliable data record. The longest data record we identified was at the COOP station "Carlsbad" (1900-present; Table 4.3), discussed previously. However, this station is 62 km northeast of GUMO and may not represent GUMO weather conditions, as it is located well away from the Guadalupe Mountains (Figure 4.1). "Cornudas Svc. Stn." is another COOP station with a longer climate record (1940-present). This station is 43 km west of GUMO and measured precipitation only until 1962. The data record at this station has become unreliable in the past 5 years.

Besides the NADP and RAWS stations identified within GUMO, only a few stations within 100 km of GUMO provide near-real-time weather data. These include the SAO stations at Pine Springs and Carlsbad, along with the RAWS stations "Batdraw" and "Queen," located northeast of GUMO (Figure 4.1; Table 4.3).

One station was identified within WHSA (Table 4.3). This is a long-term COOP station (White Sands Natl. Mon.) which is located in far eastern WHSA (Figure 4.1) and has been active since 1939. No near-real-time weather stations were identified within the park unit.

We identified 15 COOP stations within 50 km of WHSA (Table 4.3). Six of these climate stations are currently active. The COOP station "Mountain Park," located 26 km northeast of WHSA, provides the longest data record in the area (1894-present). The data record at "Mountain Park" is very complete after 1948. The COOP station "Orogrande" is southeast of WHSA and has a data record that starts in 1904. This station's data record is fairly complete. Reliable observations have been available at "Orogrande" since April 1976. Prior to this, a sizeable data gap occurred from August 1975 to March 1976, with scattered data gaps before that. The COOP station "Tularosa" has been operating since 1906. This station is 24 km northeast of WHSA. The data record at "Tularosa" has been quite complete since 1980 but is questionable in quality prior to that time. Two very complete long-term data records are provided by the COOP stations "Alamogordo" and "Jornada Exp. Range." The former station, located 21 km east of WHSA, contains the longer data record (1909-present), while the latter station (located 26 km west of WHSA) has been active since 1914.

Numerous active near-real-time stations are present within 50 km of WHSA (Table 4.3). The near-real-time stations we identified are located primarily in the Alamogordo vicinity and in the San Andres Range, south and west of WHSA (Figure 4.1). These stations are associated primarily with the RAWS and SAO networks, although some active WBAN stations were also identified. Six active RAWS stations were identified. The closest RAWS stations to the park unit are "Cosmic," 11 km east of WHSA, and "San Andres," 12 km southwest of WHSA. Although "Cosmic" began operating in 1990, data have only been reliable since April 1995. The data record from "San Andres" (1997-present) is reliable. "Mayhill," 48 km east of WHSA, provides the longest record among the active RAWS stations. However, there are issues with the data record at this site, including a large data gap from March 1996 to October 2001. Of the four active SAO stations we identified within 50 km of WHSA, "Northrup" is the closest site, 3 km north of the park unit, while the longest data records come from the SAO stations at Holloman (5 km northeast) and Las Cruces (31 km southwest). Both stations' data records go back to the 1940s.

4.2.2. Trans-Pecos and Southwestern Texas
No weather or climate stations were identified within the boundaries of AMIS (Table 4.4). The closest station to the park unit is the COOP station "Amistad Dam," located just outside the southeast boundary of AMIS (Figure 4.2). This station has a very complete data record that starts in 1964. "Langtry" is another COOP station within 1 km of AMIS. This station is located just outside the northwestern edge of AMIS. "Langtry" provides the longest data record (1897-present) among the COOP stations we identified within 50 km of AMIS. However, this data record is only reliable since September 1968. Another long-term climate record is provided at the COOP station "Pandale 1 N," which is 40 km north of AMIS and has a data record starting in 1909. This data record has scattered data gaps throughout it. Temperatures were not measured at "Pandale 1 N" until 1964. A few other active COOP stations within 50 km of AMIS have data records that go back to the 1960s.

There are very few sources of automated weather data for AMIS. The only near-real-time station we identified is the SAO station at Del Rio, Texas, which is about 20 km southeast of AMIS (Figure 4.2) and has been in operation since 1943.

Table 4.4. Weather/climate stations for the CHDN park units in Trans-Pecos and southwestern Texas. Stations inside park units and within a specified buffer distance of the park unit boundary (50 km for AMIS and FODA, 100 km for BIBE and RIGR) are included. Missing entries are indicated by "M".

Name	Lat.	Lon.	Elev. (m)	Network	Start	End	In Park?
Amistad National Recreation Area (AMIS)							
Lake Walk	29.517	-100.983	305	COOP	5/1/1949	8/31/1968	Yes
Langtry 2	29.800	-101.567	409	COOP	5/1/1958	1/31/1969	Yes
Amistad Dam	29.461	-101.029	353	COOP	1/1/1964	Present	No
Bakers Crossing	29.950	-101.150	460	COOP	M	2/29/1988	No
Brackettville	29.608	-100.474	511	COOP	4/1/1966	Present	No
Brackettville	29.317	-100.414	341	COOP	1/1/1897	10/1/2002	No
Carta Valley	29.791	-100.674	564	COOP	7/1/1963	Present	No
Comstock	29.683	-101.183	483	COOP	11/27/1903	9/30/1987	No
Comstock	29.950	-101.130	454	COOP	10/19/1995	Present	No
Comstock 11 WNW	29.700	-101.350	384	COOP	2/19/1992	3/18/1993	No
Comstock 22 NE	29.877	-100.897	488	COOP	4/1/1978	4/12/2004	No
Del Rio	29.367	-100.917	305	COOP	11/1/1905	12/31/1963	No
Del Rio	29.332	-100.930	265	COOP	1/1/1923	4/12/2004	No
Del Rio	29.367	-100.817	334	COOP	7/1/1948	9/1/1957	No
Del Rio	29.377	-100.928	304	COOP	3/1/1963	Present	No
Del Rio 2 NW	29.423	-100.911	329	COOP	4/11/1996	Present	No
Del Rio 3 S	29.333	-100.883	268	COOP	9/1/1946	2/28/1954	No
Fawcett Ranch	29.867	-100.900	458	COOP	7/1/1947	7/31/1949	No
Fort Clark	29.300	-100.450	336	COOP	5/1/1943	8/31/1944	No
Hudspeth River Ranch	29.988	-101.179	497	COOP	3/1/1988	Present	No
Juno	30.083	-101.117	555	COOP	8/20/1980	5/10/1999	No
Juno	30.150	-101.117	549	COOP	4/1/1953	5/31/1975	No
Juno 5 S	30.068	-101.110	505	COOP	4/1/1978	3/15/2004	No
Langtry	29.793	-101.560	393	COOP	7/1/1897	Present	No
Myers Ranch	29.800	-100.817	M	COOP	4/1/1940	12/31/1941	No
Pandale 1 N	30.172	-101.556	515	COOP	8/6/1909	Present	No
Pandale 11 NE	30.268	-101.453	507	COOP	11/1/1981	1/24/2003	No
Pandale Crossing	30.130	-101.570	476	COOP	4/1/1978	4/12/2004	No
Rocksprings 18 SW	29.789	-100.425	526	COOP	1/1/1963	6/30/1993	No
Rocksprings 26 SSW	29.688	-100.422	515	COOP	7/1/1995	Present	No
Del Rio	29.377	-100.928	304	SAO	3/1/1963	Present	No
Del Rio	29.367	-100.783	327	SAO	2/1/1943	Present	No
Fort Clark	29.300	-100.433	320	WBAN	5/1/1928	12/31/1931	No
Big Bend National Park (BIBE)							
K-Bar	29.302	-103.177	1052	CASTNet	9/15/1990	Present	Yes
Boquillas R.S.	29.185	-102.962	566	COOP	6/15/1910	Present	Yes
Castolon	29.134	-103.515	661	COOP	1/1/1947	Present	Yes
Chisos Basin	29.270	-103.300	1615	COOP	8/1/1943	Present	Yes
Coopers Store	29.583	-103.133	885	COOP	9/1/1943	5/31/1951	Yes
Hot Springs	29.183	-103.000	671	COOP	3/1/1939	6/30/1952	Yes
Maverick R.S.	29.283	-103.500	824	COOP	8/1/1961	5/31/1965	Yes
Panther Junction	29.327	-103.206	1140	COOP	4/1/1955	Present	Yes

Name	Lat.	Lon.	Elev. (m)	Network	Start	End	In Park?
Persimmon Gap	29.660	-103.174	873	COOP	2/1/1952	Present	Yes
K-Bar	29.302	-103.177	1052	GPMP	9/15/1990	7/4/1995	Yes
Big Bend NP-K-Bar	29.302	-103.177	1056	NADP	4/10/1980	Present	Yes
Chisos Basin	29.267	-103.300	1646	RAWS	6/1/2000	Present	Yes
Panther Junction	29.317	-103.200	1143	RAWS	4/1/2003	Present	Yes
Big Bend Ranch SP	29.437	-103.958	1262	COOP	2/1/1995	Present	No
Heath Canyon	29.448	-102.828	536	COOP	3/22/1995	Present	No
Lajitas	29.269	-103.758	732	COOP	11/1/1977	Present	No
Marathon	30.207	-103.245	1239	COOP	7/1/1896	Present	No
Marfa 16 SSE	30.133	-103.883	1421	COOP	6/1/1969	6/30/1981	No
Marfa 19 S	30.033	-104.017	1342	COOP	11/1/1950	8/31/1964	No
O 2 Ranch	29.850	-103.750	1153	COOP	2/1/1914	11/30/1928	No
One O One Ranch	30.167	-103.767	1101	COOP	3/31/1945	11/30/1950	No
Persimmon Gap 6 E	29.650	-103.083	772	COOP	9/1/1979	6/20/1985	No
Plata	29.850	-104.017	1144	COOP	8/1/1964	2/28/1977	No
Presidio	29.571	-104.370	794	COOP	10/1/1927	Present	No
Presidio 5 SE	29.552	-104.552	777	COOP	1/1/1968	6/14/2003	No
Rancho Escondido	30.017	-103.767	1464	COOP	7/1/1943	11/30/1950	No
Study Butte	29.317	-103.533	793	COOP	3/1/1923	1/31/1930	No
Study Butte	29.329	-103.553	781	COOP	4/27/1993	7/21/2006	No
Terlingua	29.300	-103.550	790	COOP	7/1/1947	5/31/1963	No
Terlingua Ranch	29.453	-103.394	1124	COOP	4/28/1993	Present	No
CW1351 Alpine	30.277	-103.580	1574	CWOP	M	Present	No
CW4135 Alpine	30.370	-103.780	1492	CWOP	M	Present	No
KB5TNP-5 Alpine	30.359	-103.662	1402	CWOP	M	Present	No
Fort Davis	30.412	-103.523	1352	WX4U	M	Present	No

Fort Davis National Historic Site (FODA)

Name	Lat.	Lon.	Elev. (m)	Network	Start	End	In Park?
Alpine	30.374	-103.663	1347	COOP	3/1/1900	Present	No
Alpine 10 SW	30.267	-103.783	1534	COOP	10/1/1971	5/31/1979	No
Alpine 11 NW	30.467	-103.767	1385	COOP	7/1/1971	9/30/1971	No
Alpine 7 NW	30.370	-103.781	1500	COOP	5/8/2006	Present	No
Antelope Springs Ranch	30.183	-103.917	1427	COOP	5/1/1940	8/31/1944	No
Balmorhea	30.984	-103.740	981	COOP	9/1/1923	Present	No
Balmorhea	30.983	-103.733	973	COOP	2/1/1949	3/31/1960	No
Balmorhea Circle H R	30.850	-103.983	1525	COOP	3/1/1953	6/30/1954	No
Balmorhea WB Pan.	31.000	-103.683	982	COOP	9/1/1946	4/30/1950	No
Bloys Campground	30.533	-104.133	1757	COOP	5/1/1968	1/31/1978	No
Childress Ranch	31.000	-104.033	M	COOP	8/1/1939	8/31/1943	No
Fort Davis	30.603	-103.886	1481	COOP	1/1/1902	Present	No
Kent 8 SE	31.017	-104.110	1440	COOP	4/1/1988	Present	No
Kingston Ranch	30.867	-103.983	1354	COOP	1/1/1941	1/31/1953	No
Marfa	30.250	-104.048	1398	COOP	10/13/1958	Present	No
Marfa	30.250	-103.883	1481	COOP	6/1/1907	8/31/1960	No
Marfa 9 W	30.300	-104.167	1449	COOP	2/1/1952	5/31/1969	No
Marfa Arpt.	30.367	-104.017	1473	COOP	7/1/1969	12/31/1980	No
Marfa Charco M R	30.483	-104.117	1615	COOP	1/1/1942	7/23/1968	No

Name	Lat.	Lon.	Elev. (m)	Network	Start	End	In Park?
Marfa Ryan	30.367	-104.317	1434	COOP	4/1/1951	4/30/1959	No
Merrill Ranch	30.533	-104.050	1668	COOP	1/1/1939	5/31/1968	No
Mount Locke	30.705	-104.023	2070	COOP	2/1/1935	Present	No
One O One Ranch	30.167	-103.767	1101	COOP	3/31/1945	11/30/1950	No
Popham Ranch	30.883	-103.550	1007	COOP	1/2/1941	1/31/1953	No
Toyahvale	30.933	-103.767	1019	COOP	7/1/1947	2/28/1949	No
CW0068 Fort Davis	30.755	-103.858	1500	CWOP	M	Present	No
CW0421 Ft. Davis	30.764	-103.850	1616	CWOP	M	Present	No
CW1351 Alpine	30.277	-103.580	1574	CWOP	M	Present	No
CW4135 Alpine	30.370	-103.780	1492	CWOP	M	Present	No
KB5TNP-5 Alpine	30.359	-103.662	1402	CWOP	M	Present	No
Davis	30.600	-103.883	1487	RAWS	2/1/2001	3/31/2004	No
Fort Davis	30.601	-103.887	1452	RAWS	1/1/2004	Present	No
Alpine	30.383	-103.683	1376	SAO	6/19/1992	Present	No
Marfa	30.250	-103.883	1481	SAO	6/1/1907	8/31/1960	No
Marfa Arpt.	30.367	-104.017	1473	SAO	7/1/1969	12/31/1980	No
Alpine	30.350	-103.667	1360	WBAN	10/1/1937	Present	No
Marfa	30.267	-103.900	1482	WBAN	4/1/1928	5/31/1959	No
Marfa Auto	30.367	-104.017	481	WBAN	M	Present	No
Fort Davis	30.412	-103.523	1352	WX4U	M	Present	No

Rio Grande Wild and Scenic River (RIGR)

Name	Lat.	Lon.	Elev. (m)	Network	Start	End	In Park?
K-Bar	29.302	-103.177	1052	CASTNet	9/15/1990	Present	No
Acton Ranch	30.352	-101.252	613	COOP	2/18/1992	Present	No
Amistad Dam	29.461	-101.029	353	COOP	1/1/1964	Present	No
Baggett Ranch	30.350	-101.033	616	COOP	4/1/1978	2/13/2003	No
Bakers Crossing	29.950	-101.150	460	COOP	M	2/29/1988	No
Bakersfield 11 SSE	30.717	-102.217	939	COOP	7/1/1980	6/30/1982	No
Big Bend Ranch SP	29.437	-103.958	1262	COOP	2/1/1995	Present	No
Boquillas R.S.	29.185	-102.962	566	COOP	6/15/1910	Present	No
Castolon	29.134	-103.515	661	COOP	1/1/1947	Present	No
Chandler Ranch	30.467	-101.717	573	COOP	4/1/1978	6/28/1991	No
Chisos Basin	29.270	-103.300	1615	COOP	8/1/1943	Present	No
Comstock	29.683	-101.183	483	COOP	11/27/1903	9/30/1987	No
Comstock	29.950	-101.130	454	COOP	10/19/1995	Present	No
Comstock 11 WNW	29.700	-101.350	384	COOP	2/19/1992	3/18/1993	No
Comstock 22 NE	29.877	-100.897	488	COOP	4/1/1978	4/12/2004	No
Coopers Store	29.583	-103.133	885	COOP	9/1/1943	5/31/1951	No
Cox Ranch 2	30.583	-101.483	671	COOP	4/1/1978	2/13/2003	No
Del Rio	29.377	-100.928	304	COOP	3/1/1963	Present	No
Del Rio	29.367	-100.917	305	COOP	11/1/1905	12/31/1963	No
Del Rio	29.332	-100.930	265	COOP	1/1/1923	4/12/2004	No
Del Rio 2 NW	29.423	-100.911	329	COOP	4/11/1996	Present	No
Del Rio 3 S	29.333	-100.883	268	COOP	9/1/1946	2/28/1954	No
Dryden	30.050	-102.117	668	COOP	5/1/1966	1/31/1995	No
Dryden 10 NE	30.200	-101.833	695	COOP	5/1/1937	9/30/1993	No
Dryden 14 S	29.833	-102.167	411	COOP	4/1/1978	Present	No

Name	Lat.	Lon.	Elev. (m)	Network	Start	End	In Park?
Fawcett Ranch	29.867	-100.900	458	COOP	7/1/1947	7/31/1949	No
Fort Stockton 25 SSW	30.533	-102.950	1251	COOP	4/1/1955	4/30/1958	No
Fort Stockton 35 SSW	30.383	-103.033	1339	COOP	4/1/1958	3/31/1987	No
Fort Stockton 38 SE	30.560	-102.365	906	COOP	1/29/2005	Present	No
Heath Canyon	29.448	-102.828	536	COOP	3/22/1995	Present	No
Hot Springs	29.183	-103.000	671	COOP	3/1/1939	6/30/1952	No
Hudspeth River Ranch	29.988	-101.179	497	COOP	3/1/1988	Present	No
Juno	30.083	-101.117	555	COOP	8/20/1980	5/10/1999	No
Juno	30.150	-101.117	549	COOP	4/1/1953	5/31/1975	No
Juno 10 NNE	30.283	-101.083	641	COOP	10/1/1975	6/30/1989	No
Juno 5 S	30.068	-101.110	505	COOP	4/1/1978	3/15/2004	No
Lajitas	29.269	-103.758	732	COOP	11/1/1977	Present	No
Lake Walk	29.517	-100.983	305	COOP	5/1/1949	8/31/1968	No
Langtry	29.793	-101.560	393	COOP	7/1/1897	Present	No
Langtry 2	29.800	-101.567	409	COOP	5/1/1958	1/31/1969	No
Marathon	30.207	-103.245	1239	COOP	7/1/1896	Present	No
Maverick R.S.	29.283	-103.500	824	COOP	8/1/1961	5/31/1965	No
Myers Ranch	29.800	-100.817	M	COOP	4/1/1940	12/31/1941	No
Ozona 23 SW	30.583	-102.167	M	COOP	M	Present	No
Pandale 1 N	30.172	-101.556	515	COOP	8/6/1909	Present	No
Pandale 11 NE	30.268	-101.453	507	COOP	11/1/1981	1/24/2003	No
Pandale Crossing	30.130	-101.570	476	COOP	4/1/1978	4/12/2004	No
Panther Junction	29.327	-103.206	1140	COOP	4/1/1955	Present	No
Persimmon Gap	29.660	-103.174	873	COOP	2/1/1952	Present	No
Persimmon Gap 6 E	29.650	-103.083	772	COOP	9/1/1979	6/20/1985	No
Sanderson	30.146	-102.399	870	COOP	1/1/1897	Present	No
Sanderson 1 S	30.142	-102.384	825	COOP	2/1/1977	8/8/2006	No
Sanderson 5 NNW	30.216	-102.416	939	COOP	7/1/1947	Present	No
Sheffield	30.689	-101.827	663	COOP	10/17/1938	Present	No
Study Butte	29.317	-103.533	793	COOP	3/1/1923	1/31/1930	No
Study Butte	29.329	-103.553	781	COOP	4/27/1993	7/21/2006	No
Terlingua	29.300	-103.550	790	COOP	7/1/1947	5/31/1963	No
Terlingua Ranch	29.453	-103.394	1124	COOP	4/28/1993	Present	No
K-Bar	29.302	-103.177	1052	GPMP	9/15/1990	7/4/1995	No
Big Bend NP-K-Bar	29.302	-103.177	1056	NADP	4/10/1980	Present	No
Chisos Basin	29.267	-103.300	1646	RAWS	6/1/2000	Present	No
Panther Junction	29.317	-103.200	1143	RAWS	4/1/2003	Present	No
Del Rio	29.377	-100.928	304	SAO	3/1/1963	Present	No
Dryden	30.048	-102.213	708	SAO	6/15/1999	Present	No
Sanderson Auto	30.167	-102.417	865	SAO	M	Present	No
Dryden	30.050	-102.217	662	WBAN	5/1/1928	8/31/1936	No

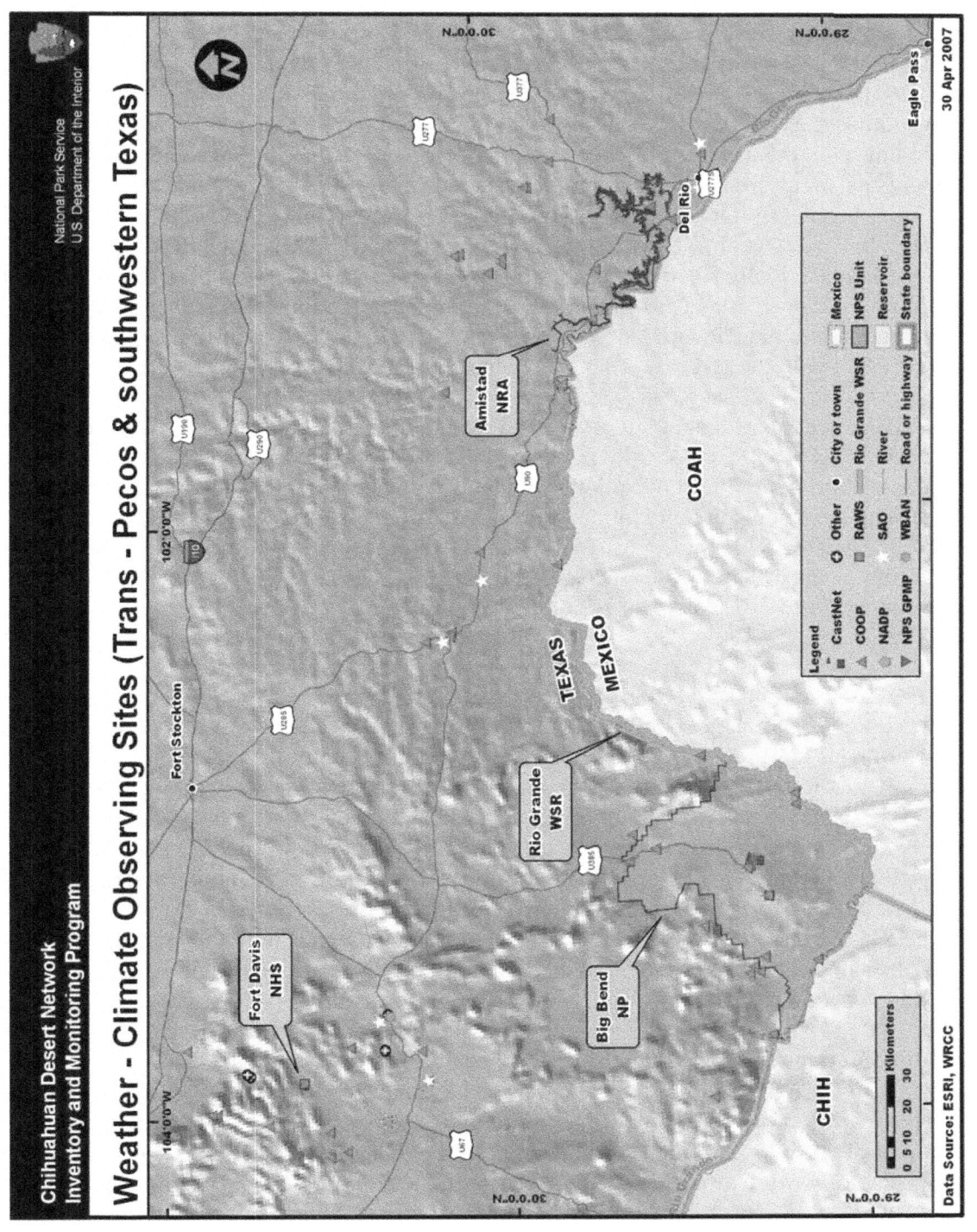

Figure 4.2. Station locations for the CHDN park units in Trans-Pecos and southwestern Texas.

37

Thirteen stations were identified within the boundaries of BIBE (Table 4.4). Nine of these stations are active, including five long-term COOP stations and at least three near-real-time stations. The near-real-time stations in the park unit include the CASTNet station "K-Bar" and two RAWS stations ("Chisos Basin" and "Panther Junction"), all located in central BIBE (Figure 4.2). The data record at the RAWS station "Chisos Basin" has a data gap in June 2005 but is otherwise complete. The active COOP stations we identified in BIBE have data records that all start in the 1950s or earlier. The longest data record is at "Boquillas R.S.," located along the Rio Grande in southeastern BIBE. The data record at this station goes back to 1910. However, precipitation measurements have only been reliably complete since the 1950s and temperature measurements have only been reliably complete since the 1980s. Very complete data records are available from the COOP stations "Chisos Basin" (1943-present) and "Panther Junction" (1955-present), both located in central BIBE. The data record at the COOP station "Persimmon Gap" (1952-present), located in northern BIBE, has only been reliable since 1981. There are scattered data gaps at this site even after 1981. The COOP station "Persimmon Gap" (1952-present), which is located along the Rio Grande in southwestern BIBE, has had a fairly complete data record since 1980, with the last major data gap occurring in April 2005.

Outside of BIBE, we identified mostly COOP stations, although a few near-real-time stations associated with the CWOP and WX4U networks were also identified, primarily near the town of Alpine, Texas. Six of the 17 COOP stations we identified within 100 km of BIBE are active (Table 4.2). The longest data record among the active COOP stations comes from "Marathon" (1896-present), located 57 km north of BIBE. This site has generally had unreliable data, however, with numerous data gaps, especially before 1940. The COOP station "Presidio," located 68 km west of BIBE, has a fairly complete data record, with only occasional small data gaps.

No weather/climate stations have been identified within the boundaries of FODA (Table 4.4). The closest source of climate data for FODA comes from the COOP station "Fort Davis," just outside the boundary of FODA (Figure 4.2). This station has been operating since 1902 but measured only precipitation until 1981, when temperature observations began. There is a large data gap at this station from December 1974 until June 1981; otherwise, the data record is fairly complete, with only occasional small data gaps. The COOP station "Mount Locke" provides a very complete data record (1935-present) 16 km northwest of FODA. The longest data record we identified within 50 km of FODA is at the COOP station "Alpine," located 33 km southeast of FODA. The data record at this station has occasional small data gaps but otherwise is fairly complete. The same can be said of the data record at the COOP station "Balmorhea" (1923-present), which is 44 km north of FODA.

Near-real-time stations associated with several weather networks were identified within 50 km of FODA. One active RAWS station (Fort Davis) was identified just outside FODA (Figure 4.2), providing the main source of near-real-time weather data for the park unit. The only active SAO station we identified was at Alpine, 31 km southeast of FODA. Several stations with the CWOP and WX4U networks were also identified, primarily in the communities of Alpine and Fort Davis. Two active WBAN stations were also identified, one in Alpine and the other in Marfa (28 km southwest of FODA).

No weather/climate stations have been identified within RIGR (Table 4.4). The closest station to RIGR is the COOP station "Heath Canyon," just outside the boundary of RIGR. This station has been operating since 1995. The COOP station "Marathon," discussed previously, is 75 km northwest of RIGR and provides the longest data record among the active COOP stations we identified for RIGR. The COOP station "Sanderson" is 31 km north of RIGR. The data record at this station is very complete since March 1948 for precipitation and since August 1961 for temperature. The data record at "Sanderson" was unreliable before 1948. Other long-term records are provided by the COOP stations "Langtry" (1897-present; 19 km north), "Pandale 1 N" (1909-present; 48 km northeast), and "Boquillas R.S." (1910-present), all of which have been discussed previously. We identified numerous other COOP stations having data records extending back to the 1930s and 1940s.

The closest source of near-real-time weather data for RIGR is the SAO station "Dryden," located 21 km north of RIGR. This station has been operating since 1999. Other SAO stations we identified for RIGR are "Del Rio" and "Sanderson Auto." The two RAWS stations in BIBE ("Chisos Basin" and "Panther Junction") also provide near-real-time data for RIGR.

5.0. Conclusions and Recommendations

We have based our findings on an examination of available climate records within CHDN units, discussions with NPS staff and other collaborators, and prior knowledge of the area. Here, we offer an evaluation and general comments pertaining to the status, prospects, and needs for climate-monitoring capabilities in CHDN.

5.1. Chihuahuan Desert Inventory and Monitoring Network

As Reid and Reiser (2006) and Reiser et al. (2006) point out, current coverage of weather/climate stations within the CHDN is unsatisfactory for ongoing ecological monitoring efforts within much of the network. The variability in precipitation in the CHDN desert locations, particularly during the monsoon season, is a constant impediment to properly interpreting results from biological research activities in the region (Reid and Reiser 2006). Unfortunately, there is currently very little data available that would permit a better understanding of precipitation patterns within the CHDN. The weather and climate stations that have been identified are mostly located near visitor centers and other areas with higher visitor concentration. Very little of the desert environment is sampled away from these locations. Sparse station coverage is also fairly common outside of most of the CHDN park units, forcing CHDN weather and climate monitoring efforts to sometimes look to distant sources (e.g., Indio Mountain Research Station) and even international sources (e.g., Mexico stations) for data.

5.1.1. CAVE and GUMO

The majority of stations we have identified for CAVE and GUMO are concentrated near the visitor centers, both located in the eastern portions of the park units. Weather monitoring efforts in these park units could benefit greatly by installing one remote near-real-time station, such as RAWS, in the western portions of both park units. This could be especially beneficial for GUMO, due to the great heterogeneity of ecotypes within the park unit that currently remain unsampled for weather/climate conditions.

5.1.2. WHSA

Like CAVE and GUMO, the weather/climate stations within WHSA are situated at or near the main visitor center. Since WHSA has not emphasized the need for climate monitoring within its boundaries as strongly as other CHDN park units, the current lack of station coverage, particularly regarding near-real-time stations, does not appear to be an issue. However, as WHSA must rely heavily on outside sources of weather and climate data, climate monitoring efforts for WHSA will benefit if the park unit works with local agencies to encourage the continued operation of long-term stations (e.g., Jornada Experimental Range) and near-real-time stations (RAWS and SAO) that are around the park unit. Fortunately these stations are fairly plentiful around WHSA.

5.1.3. AMIS, BIBE, and RIGR

While having several available sources of long-term climate records in and near the park unit, AMIS currently lacks any near-real-time weather stations. The SAO station at Del Rio is currently the only source of near-real-time weather data for the park unit. If resources allow, AMIS may want to consider installing an automated station (such as RAWS) at Amistad Dam, to complement the existing COOP station. Another option would be to install such a station along the Rio Grande somewhere at the western edge of AMIS, which would not only benefit weather monitoring efforts in AMIS, but also provide an eastern data point for monitoring near-real-time weather conditions in RIGR. A western data point for RIGR could also be provided by installing a near-real-time station like RAWS at one of the existing COOP stations in BIBE (e.g., "Boquillas R.S." or "Castolon"). Near-real-time weather monitoring efforts in BIBE, which currently has little automated station coverage away from the main visitor centers (e.g., Chisos Basin and Panther Junction), could be greatly improved by adding such a station along the Rio Grande. By adding near-real-time stations at both the west and east ends of RIGR, some of the climate monitoring needs for RIGR could begin to be addressed while simultaneously keeping the main portion of RIGR free from additional man-made structures, in accordance with the mission of being a wild and scenic riverway.

5.2. Spatial Variations in Mean Climate

Precipitation across the CHDN is predominantly convective in nature, associated with summertime thunderstorm activity. This causes precipitation over the CHDN region to be highly variable over short horizontal distances. In the western portions of CHDN, topography also introduces considerable fine-scale structure to mean climate (temperature and precipitation). Issues encountered in mapping mean climate are discussed in Appendix D and in Redmond et al. (2005).

For areas where new stations will be installed, if only a few new stations will be emplaced, the primary goal should be overall characterization of the main climate elements (temperature and precipitation and their joint relative, snow). This level of characterization generally requires that (a) stations should not be located in deep valley bottoms (cold air drainage pockets) or near excessively steep slopes and (b) stations should be distributed spatially in the major biomes of each park. If such stations already are present in the vicinity, then additional stations would be best used for two important and somewhat competing purposes: (a) add redundancy as backup for loss of data from current stations (or loss of the physical stations) or (b) provide added information on spatial heterogeneity in climate arising from topographic diversity.

5.3. Climate Change Detection

There is much interest in the adaptation of CHDN ecosystems in response to possible future climate change. In particular, there are concerns about the potential impact of global warming on species extinctions and the ability of species to adapt to future climate changes. If temperatures continue to warm and montane habitats shrink, as expected, local extinction of some species is likely.

The desire for credible, accurate, complete, and long-term climate records—from any location—cannot be overemphasized. Thus, this consideration always should have a high priority. However, because of spatial diversity in climate, monitoring that fills knowledge gaps and provides information on long-term temporal variability in short-distance relationships also will be valuable. We cannot be sure that climate variability and climate change will affect all parts of a given park unit equally. In fact, it is appropriate to speculate that this is not the case, and spatial variations in temporal variability extend to small spatial scales, a consequence of diversity within CHDN in both topography and in land use patterns.

5.4. Aesthetics

This issue arises frequently enough to deserve comment. Standards for quality climate measurements require open exposures away from heat sources, buildings, pavement, close vegetation and tall trees, and human intrusion (thus away from property lines). By their nature, sites that meet these standards are usually quite visible. These sites are also quite rare, making them precisely the same places that managers wish to protect from aesthetic intrusion. The most suitable and scientifically defensible sites frequently are rejected as candidate locations for weather/climate stations. Most weather/climate stations, therefore, tend to be "hidden" but many of these hidden locations have inferior exposures. Some measure of compromise is nearly always called for in siting weather and climate stations.

The public has vast interest and curiosity in weather and climate, and within the NPS I&M networks, such measurements consistently rate near or at the top of desired public information. There seem to be many possible opportunities for exploiting and embracing this widespread interest within the interpretive mission of the NPS. One way to do this would be to highlight rather than hide these stations and educate the public about the need for adequate siting. A number of weather displays we have encountered during visits have proven inadvertently to serve as counterexamples for how measurements should not be made.

5.5. Information Access

Access to information promotes its use, which in turn promotes attention to station care and maintenance, better data, and more use. An end-to-end view that extends from sensing to decision support is far preferable to isolated and disconnected activities and aids the support infrastructure that is ultimately so necessary for successful, long-term climate monitoring.

Decisions about improvements in monitoring capacity are facilitated greatly by the ability to examine available climate information. Various methods are being created at WRCC to improve access to that information. Web pages providing historic and ongoing climate data, and information from CHDN park units can be accessed at http://www.wrcc.dri.edu/nps. In the event that this URL changes, there still will be links from the main WRCC Web page entitled "Projects" under NPS.

The WRCC has been steadily developing software to summarize data from hourly sites. This has been occurring under the aegis of the RAWS program and a growing array of product generators ranging from daily and monthly data lists to wind roses and hourly frequency distributions. All park data are available to park personnel via an access code (needed only for data listings) that can be acquired by request. The WRCC RAWS Web page is located at http://www.wrcc.dri.edu/wraws or http://www.raws.dri.edu.

Web pages have been developed to provide access not only to historic and ongoing climate data and information from CHDN park units but also to climate-monitoring efforts for CHDN. These pages can be found through http://www.wrcc.dri.edu/nps.

Additional access to more standard climate information is accessible though the previously mentioned Web pages, as well as through http://www.wrcc.dri.edu/summary. These summaries are generally for COOP stations.

5.6. Summarized Conclusions and Recommendations

- Weather/climate station coverage in the CHDN is generally inadequate for current vital signs monitoring activities.
- Precipitation within CHDN is generally convective in nature and thus quite variable spatially and temporally, underscoring need for improved station coverage.
- Installing a near-real-time station in the western portions of both GUMO and CAVE could improve climate monitoring efforts in both park units, which currently only have stations near main visitor centers.
- Climate monitoring efforts in WHSA have not been emphasized as strongly as for other CHDN park units. Since WHSA must rely on outside sources of weather/climate data, such as Jornada Experimental Range, WHSA could encourage local agencies responsible for those stations to continue their operation.
- Near-real-time weather data is currently limited for AMIS. AMIS may want to consider installing an automated station (e.g., RAWS) at either Amistad Dam or along the Rio Grande in western AMIS.
- Automated weather station coverage in BIBE is currently limited primarily to visitor centers in central and northern BIBE. The park unit may consider installing one remote near-real-time station (e.g. RAWS) at one of the existing COOP stations along the Rio Grande (Boquillas R.S.; Castolon).
- Proposed installations in AMIS and BIBE could also benefit near-real-time weather monitoring efforts for RIGR, providing both eastern and western data points for the riverway.

6.0 Literature Cited

Adams, D. K., and A. C. Comrie. 1997. The North American Monsoon. Bulletin of the American Meteorological Society, **78**:2197-2213.

American Association of State Climatologists. 1985. Heights and exposure standards for sensors on automated weather stations. The State Climatologist **9**.

Archer, S. 1994. Woody plant encroachment into southwestern grasslands and savannas: rates, patterns and proximate causes. Pages 13–68 *in* M. Vavra, W. A. Laycock, and R. D. Pieper, editors. Ecological implications of livestock herbivory in the west. Society for Range Management, Denver, Colorado.

Bailey, R. G. 1995. Description of the ecoregions of the United States, 2nd edition. USDA Forest Service, Washington, D.C. Miscellaneous Publication 1391.

Bevis, M., S. Businger, T. A. Herring, C. Rocken, R. A. Anthes, and R. H. Ware. 1992. GPS meteorology: remote sensing of the atmospheric water vapor using the global positioning system. Journal of Geophysical Research **97**:75–94.

Bonan, G. B. 2002. Ecological Climatology: Concepts and Applications. Cambridge University Press.

Bureau of Land Management. 1997. Remote Automatic Weather Station (RAWS) and Remote Environmental Monitoring Systems (REMS) standards. RAWS/REMS Support Facility, Boise, Idaho.

Chapin III, F. S., M. S. Torn, and M. Tateno. 1996. Principles of ecosystem sustainability. The American Naturalist **148**:1016-1037.

Daly, C., R. P. Neilson, and D. L. Phillips. 1994. A statistical-topographic model for mapping climatological precipitation over mountainous terrain. Journal of Applied Meteorology **33**:140-158.

Daly, C., W. P. Gibson, G. H. Taylor, G. L. Johnson, and P. Pasteris. 2002. A knowledge-based approach to the statistical mapping of climate. Climate Research **22**:99-113.

Dick-Peddie, W. A. 1993. New Mexico Vegetation: past, present, and future. University of New Mexico Press, Albuquerque, New Mexico.

Dinerstein E., D. Olson, J. Atchley, C. Loucks, S. Contreras-Balderas, R. Abell, E. Indigo, E. Enkerlin, C. E. William, and G. Castelleja. 2000. Ecoregion-based conservation in the Chihuahuan Desert, a biological assessment. World Wildlife Fund.

Doggett, M., C. Daly, J. Smith, W. Gibson, G. Taylor, G. Johnson, and P. Pasteris. 2004. High-resolution 1971-2000 mean monthly temperature maps for the western United States.

Fourteenth AMS Conf. on Applied Climatology, 84th AMS Annual Meeting. Seattle, Washington, American Meteorological Society, Boston, Massachusetts, January 2004, Paper 4.3, CD-ROM.

Douglas M. W., R. Maddox, K. Howard, and S. Reyes. 1993. The Mexican Monsoon. Journal of Climate **6**:1665-1667.

Duan, J., M. Bevis, P. Fang, Y. Bock, S. Chiswell, S. Businger, C. Rocken, F. Solheim, T. van Hove, R. Ware, and others. 1996. GPS meteorology: direct estimation of the absolute value of precipitable water. Journal of Applied Meteorology **35**:830-838.

Ehleringer, J. R., R. F. Sage, L. B. Flanagan, and R. W. Pearcy. 1991. Climate change and the evolution of C4 photosynthesis. Trends in Ecology and Evolution **6**:95–99.

Environmental Protection Agency. 1987. On-site meteorological program guidance for regulatory modeling applications. EPA-450/4-87-013. Environmental Protection Agency, Office of Air Quality Planning and Standards, Research Triangle Park, North Carolina.

Finklin, A. I., and W. C. Fischer. 1990. Weather station handbook –an interagency guide for wildland managers. NFES No. 2140. National Wildfire Coordinating Group, Boise, Idaho.

Gibson, W. P., C. Daly, T. Kittel, D. Nychka, C. Johns, N. Rosenbloom, A. McNab, and G. Taylor. 2002. Development of a 103-year high-resolution climate data set for the conterminous United States. Thirteenth AMS Conf. on Applied Climatology. Portland, Oregon, American Meteorological Society, Boston, MA, May 2002:181-183.

Gillette, D. A., and A. M. Pitchford. 2004. Sand flux in the northern Chihuahuan desert, New Mexico, USA, and the influence of mesquite-dominated landscapes. Journal of Geophysical Research-Earth Surface **109**:3.

Groeger, A. W., and D. Bass. 2005. Empirical predictions of water temperatures in a subtropical reservoir. Archiv für Hydrobiologie **162**:267–285.

Hastings, J. R., and R. M. Turner. 1965. The changing mile: an ecological study of vegetation change with time in the lower mile of an arid and semi-arid region. University of Arizona Press, Tucson, Arizona.

I&M. 2006. I&M Inventories home page. http://science.nature.nps.gov/im/inventory/index.cfm.

Jacobson, M. C., R. J. Charlson, H. Rodhe, and G. H. Orians. 2000. Earth System Science: From Biogeochemical Cycles to Global Change. Academic Press, San Diego.

Karl, T. R., V. E. Derr, D. R. Easterling, C. K. Folland, D. J. Hoffman, S. Levitus, N. Nicholls, D. E. Parker, and G. W. Withee. 1996. Critical issues for long-term climate monitoring. Pages 55-92 *in* T. R. Karl, editor. Long Term Climate Monitoring by the Global Climate Observing System, Kluwer Publishing.

Monger, H. C., and B. T. Bestelmeyer. 2006. The soil-geomorphic template and biotic change in arid and semi-arid ecosystems. Journal of Arid Environments **65**:207–218.

National Assessment Synthesis Team. 2001. Climate Change Impacts on the United States: The Potential Consequences of Climate Variability and Change, Report for the U.S. Global Change Research Program. Cambridge University Press, Cambridge, UK.

National Research Council. 2001. A Climate Services Vision: First Steps Toward the Future. National Academies Press, Washington, D.C.

National Wildfire Coordinating Group. 2004. National fire danger rating system weather station standards. Report PMS 426.3. National Wildfire Coordinating Group, Boise, Idaho.

Neilson, R. P. 1987. Biotic regionalization and climatic controls in western North America. Vegetatio **70**:135-147.

Noy-Meir, I. 1973. Desert ecosystems: Environment and producers. Annual Review of Ecology and Systematics **4**:25-51.

Oakley, K. L., L. P. Thomas, and S. G. Fancy. 2003. Guidelines for long-term monitoring protocols. Wildlife Society Bulletin **31**:1000-1003.

Okin, G. S., D. A. Gillette, and J. E. Herrick. 2006. Multi-scale controls on and consequences of Aeolian processes in landscape change in arid and semi-arid environments. Journal of Arid Environments **65**:253–275.

Osmond, C. B., M. Austin, J. Berry, W. Billings, J. Boyer, J. Dacey, P. Nobel, S. Smith, and W. Winner. 1987. Stress physiology and the distribution of plants. BioScience **37**:38–48.

Peters, D. P. C., B. T. Bestelmeyer, J. E. Herrick, E. L. Frederickson, H. C. Monger, and K. M. Havstad. 2006. Disentangling complex landscapes: new insights into arid and semiarid system dynamics. BioScience **56**:491–501.

Pigott, C. D., and S. Pigott. 1993. Water as a determinant of the distribution of trees at the boundary of the Mediterranean zone. Journal of Applied Ecology **81**:557–566.

Redmond, K. T., D. B. Simeral, and G. D. McCurdy. 2005. Climate monitoring for southwest Alaska national parks: network design and site selection. Report 05-01. Western Regional Climate Center, Reno, Nevada.

Reid, W. H. and M. H. Reiser. 2006. General summary on the climate of Chihuahuan Desert network parks and some nearby protected lands. Chihuahuan Desert Network, Las Cruces, New Mexico.

Reiser, M. H., J. P. Ward, Jr., J. T. Richie, and M. A. Powell. 2006. Chihuahuan Desert Network Vital Signs Monitoring Plan: Phase II. National Park Service, Chihuahuan Desert Network, Las Cruces, New Mexico.

Reynolds, J. F., P. R. Kemp, K. Ogle, and R. J. Fernandez. 2004. Modifying the 'pulse-reserve' paradigm for deserts of North America: precipitation pulses, soil water, and plant responses. Oecologia **141**:194-210.

Rodriguez-Iturbe, I. 2000. Ecohydrology: A hydrologic perspective of climate-soil-vegetation dynamics. Water Resources Research **36**:3-9.

Ropelewski, C. F., D. S. Gutzler, R. W. Higgins, and C. R. Mechoso. 2005. The North American Monsoon System. Naval Postgraduate School, School of Engineering and Applied Sciences. Regional Monsoon Topics, Review Topic A-4. 12 pp.

Schlesinger, W. H. 1997. Biogeochemistry: An Analysis of Global Change. Academic Press, San Diego.

Schlesinger, W. H., S. L. Tartowski, and S. M. Schmidt. 2006. Nutrient cycling within an arid ecosystem. Pages 133–149 *in* K. M. Havstad, L. F. Heunneke, and W. H. Schlesinger, editors. Structure and function of a Chihuahuan Desert ecosystem. Oxford University Press, New York, New York.

Schmidt, R. H., Jr. 1979. A climatic delineation of the "real" Chihuahuan Desert. Journal of Arid Environments **2**:243-250.

Schmidt, R. H., Jr. 1990. The Mega-Chihuahuan Desert. Pages 105-115 *in* Powell, A. M., R. R. Hollander, J. C. Barlow, W. B. McGillivray, and D. J. Schmidly, editors. Symposium on Resources of the Chihuahuan Desert Region: Chihuahuan Desert Research Institute.

Schmidt, R. H., Jr., 1995. The climate of Trans-Pecos Texas. Pages 122-137 *in* Norwine, J. R., G. R. North, J. B. Valez, and J. R. Giardino, editors. Changing Climate of Texas: Predictability and Implications for the Future. GeoBooks, Texas A & M University, College Station, Texas.

Schulze, E. D., R. Robichaux, J. Grace, P. Rundel, and J. Ehleringer. 1987. Plant water balance. BioScience **37**:30–37.

Snyder, K. A., and S. L. Tartowski. 2006. Multi-scale temporal variation in water availability: implications for vegetation dynamics in arid and semi-arid ecosystems. Journal of Arid Environments **65**:219–234.

Swetnam, T. W., and J. L. Betancourt. 1990. Fire-southern oscillation relations in the southwestern United States. Science **249**:1017–1021.

Tanner, B. D. 1990. Automated weather stations. Remote Sensing Reviews **5**:73-98.

Weltzin, J. F., and G. R. McPherson. 1995. Potential effects of climate change on lower treelines in the southwestern United States. Pages 180–193 *in* L. F. Debano, P. F. Ffolliott, A. Ortega-Rubio, G. J. Gottfried, R. H. Hamre, and C. B. Edminster, technical coordinators. Biodiversity and management of the Madrean Archipelago: The Sky Islands of the southwestern United States and northwestern Mexico. USDA Forest Service General Technical Report RM-GTR-264.

Whitford, W. G., 2002. Ecology of desert systems. Academic Press, San Diego, California.

World Meteorological Organization. 1983. Guide to meteorological instruments and methods of observation, No. 8, 5th edition, World Meteorological Organization, Geneva Switzerland.

World Meteorological Organization. 2005. Organization and planning of intercomparisons of rainfall intensity gauges. World Meteorological Organization, Geneva Switzerland.

York, J. C., and W. A. Dick-Peddie. 1969. Vegetation changes in southern New Mexico during the past hundred years. Pages 157–199 *in* W. G. McGinnies and B. J. Goldman, editors. Arid lands in perspective. University of Arizona Press, Tucson, Arizona.

Yuan, L. L., R. A. Anthes, R. H. Ware, C. Rocken, W. D. Bonner, M. G. Bevis, and S. Businger. 1993. Sensing climate change using the global positioning system. Journal of Geophysical Research **98**:14925-14937.

Appendix A. Glossary

Climate—Complete and entire ensemble of statistical descriptors of temporal and spatial properties comprising the behavior of the atmosphere. These descriptors include means, variances, frequency distributions, autocorrelations, spatial correlations and other patterns of association, temporal lags, and element-to-element relationships. The descriptors have a physical basis in flows and reservoirs of energy and mass. Climate and weather phenomena shade gradually into each other and are ultimately inseparable.

Climate Element—(same as Weather Element) Attribute or property of the state of the atmosphere that is measured, estimated, or derived. Examples of climate elements include temperature, wind speed, wind direction, precipitation amount, precipitation type, relative humidity, dewpoint, solar radiation, snow depth, soil temperature at a given depth, etc. A derived element is a function of other elements (like degree days or number of days with rain) and is not measured directly with a sensor. The terms "parameter" or "variable" are not used to describe elements.

Climate Network—Group of climate stations having a common purpose; the group is often owned and maintained by a single organization.

Climate Station—Station where data are collected to track atmospheric conditions over the long-term. Often, this station operates to additional standards to verify long-term consistency. For these stations, the detailed circumstances surrounding a set of measurements (siting and exposure, instrument changes, etc.) are important.

Data—Measurements specifying the state of the physical environment. Does not include metadata.

Data Inventory—Information about overall data properties for each station within a weather or climate network. A data inventory may include start/stop dates, percentages of available data, breakdowns by climate element, counts of actual data values, counts or fractions of data types, etc. These properties must be determined by actually reading the data and thus require the data to be available, accessible, and in a readable format.

NPS I&M Network—A set of NPS park units grouped by a common theme, typically by natural resource and/or geographic region.

Metadata—Information necessary to interpret environmental data properly, organized as a history or series of snapshots—data about data. Examples include details of measurement processes, station circumstances and exposures, assumptions about the site, network purpose and background, types of observations and sensors, pre-treatment of data, access information, maintenance history and protocols, observational methods, archive locations, owner, and station start/end period.

Quality Assurance—Planned and systematic set of activities to provide adequate confidence that products and services are resulting in credible and correct information. Includes quality control.

Quality Control—Evaluation, assessment, and improvement of imperfect data by utilizing other imperfect data.

Station Inventory—Information about a set of stations obtained from metadata that accompany the network or networks. A station inventory can be compiled from direct and indirect reports prepared by others.

Weather—Instantaneous state of the atmosphere at any given time, mainly with respect to its effects on biological activities. As distinguished from climate, weather consists of the short-term (minutes to days) variations in the atmosphere. Popularly, weather is thought of in terms of temperature, precipitation, humidity, wind, sky condition, visibility, and cloud conditions.

Weather Element (same as Climate Element)—Attribute or property of the state of the atmosphere that is measured, estimated, or derived. Examples of weather elements include temperature, wind speed, wind direction, precipitation amount, precipitation type, relative humidity, dewpoint, solar radiation, snow depth, soil temperature at a given depth, etc. A derived weather element is a function of other elements (like degree days or number of days with rain) and is not measured directly. The terms "parameter" and "variable" are not used to describe weather elements.

Weather Network—Group of weather stations usually owned and maintained by a particular organization and usually for a specific purpose.

Weather Station—Station where collected data are intended for near-real-time use with less need for reference to long-term conditions. In many cases, the detailed circumstances of a set of measurements (siting and exposure, instrument changes, etc.) from weather stations are not as important as for climate stations.

Appendix B. Climate-monitoring principles

Since the late 1990s, frequent references have been made to a set of climate-monitoring principles enunciated in 1996 by Tom Karl, director of the NOAA NCDC in Asheville, North Carolina. These monitoring principles also have been referred to informally as the "Ten Commandments of Climate Monitoring." Both versions are given here. In addition, these principles have been adopted by the Global Climate Observing System (GCOS 2004).

(Compiled by Kelly Redmond, Western Regional Climate Center, Desert Research Institute, August 2000.)

B.1. Full Version (Karl et al. 1996)

B.1.1. Effects on climate records of instrument changes, observing practices, observation locations, sampling rates, etc., must be known before such changes are implemented. This can be ascertained through a period where overlapping measurements from old and new observing systems are collected or sometimes by comparing the old and new observing systems with a reference standard. Site stability for in situ measurements, both in terms of physical location and changes in the nearby environment, also should be a key criterion in site selection. Thus, many synoptic network stations, which are primarily used in weather forecasting but also provide valuable climate data, and dedicated climate stations intended to be operational for extended periods must be subject to this policy.

B.1.2. Processing algorithms and changes in these algorithms must be well documented. Documentation should be carried with the data throughout the data-archiving process.

B.1.3. Knowledge of instrument, station, and/or platform history is essential for interpreting and using the data. Changes in instrument sampling time, local environmental conditions for in situ measurements, and other factors pertinent to interpreting the observations and measurements should be recorded as a mandatory part in the observing routine and be archived with the original data.

B.1.4. In situ and other observations with a long, uninterrupted record should be maintained. Every effort should be applied to protect the data sets that have provided long-term, homogeneous observations. "Long-term" for space-based measurements is measured in decades, but for more conventional measurements, "long-term" may be a century or more. Each element in the observational system should develop a list of prioritized sites or observations based on their contribution to long-term climate monitoring.

B.1.5. Calibration, validation, and maintenance facilities are critical requirements for long-term climatic data sets. Homogeneity in the climate record must be assessed routinely, and corrective action must become part of the archived record.

B.1.6. Where feasible, some level of "low-technology" backup to "high-technology" observing systems should be developed to safeguard against unexpected operational failures.

B.1.7. Regions having insufficient data, variables and regions sensitive to change, and key measurements lacking adequate spatial and temporal resolution should be given the highest priority in designing and implementing new climate-observing systems.

B.1.8. Network designers and instrument engineers must receive long-term climate requirements at the outset of the network design process. This is particularly important because most observing systems have been designed for purposes other than long-term climate monitoring. Instruments must possess adequate accuracy with biases small enough to document climate variations and changes.

B.1.9. Much of the development of new observational capabilities and the evidence supporting the value of these observations stem from research-oriented needs or programs. A lack of stable, long-term commitment to these observations and lack of a clear transition plan from research to operations are two frequent limitations in the development of adequate, long-term monitoring capabilities. Difficulties in securing a long-term commitment must be overcome in order to improve the climate-observing system in a timely manner with minimal interruptions.

B.1.10. Data management systems that facilitate access, use, and interpretation are essential. Freedom of access, low cost, mechanisms that facilitate use (directories, catalogs, browse capabilities, availability of metadata on station histories, algorithm accessibility and documentation, etc.) and quality control should guide data management. International cooperation is critical for successful management of data used to monitor long-term climate change and variability.

B.2. Abbreviated version, "Ten Commandments of Climate Monitoring"

B.2.1. Assess the impact of new climate-observing systems or changes to existing systems before they are implemented.

"Thou shalt properly manage network change." (assess effects of proposed changes)

B.2.2. Require a suitable period where measurement from new and old climate-observing systems will overlap.

"Thou shalt conduct parallel testing." (compare old and replacement systems)

B.2.3. Treat calibration, validation, algorithm-change, and data-homogeneity assessments with the same care as the data.

"Thou shalt collect metadata." (fully document system and operating procedures)

B.2.4. Verify capability for routinely assessing the quality and homogeneity of the data including high-resolution data for extreme events.

"Thou shalt assure data quality and continuity." (assess as part of routine operating procedures)

B.2.5. Integrate assessments like those conducted by the International Panel on Climate Change into global climate-observing priorities.

"Thou shalt anticipate the use of data." (integrated environmental assessment; component in operational plan for system)

B.2.6. Maintain long-term weather and climate stations.

"Thou shalt worship historic significance." (maintain homogeneous data sets from long–term, climate-observing systems)

B.2.7. Place high priority on increasing observations in regions lacking sufficient data and in regions sensitive to change and variability.

"Thou shalt acquire complementary data." (new sites to fill observational gaps)

B.2.8. Provide network operators, designers, and instrument engineers with long-term requirements at the outset of the design and implementation phases for new systems.

"Thou shalt specify requirements for climate observation systems." (application and usage of observational data)

B.2.9. Carefully consider the transition from research-observing system to long-term operation.

"Thou shalt have continuity of purpose." (stable long-term commitments)

B.2.10. Focus on data-management systems that facilitate access, use, and interpretation of weather data and metadata.

"Thou shalt provide access to data and metadata." (readily available weather and climate information)

B.3. Literature Cited

Karl, T. R., V. E. Derr, D. R. Easterling, C. K. Folland, D. J. Hoffman, S. Levitus, N. Nicholls, D. E. Parker, and G. W. Withee. 1996. Critical Issues for Long-Term Climate Monitoring. Pages 55-92 *in* T. R. Karl, editor. Long Term Climate Monitoring by the Global Climate Observing System, Kluwer Publishing.

Global Climate Observing System. 2004. Implementation Plan for the Global Observing System for Climate in Support of the UNFCCC. GCOS-92, WMO/TD No. 1219, World Meteorological Organization, Geneva, Switzerland.

Appendix C. Factors in operating a weather/ climate network

C.1. Climate versus Weather

- Climate measurements require *consistency through time.*

C.2. Network Purpose

- Anticipated or desired lifetime.
- Breadth of network mission (commitment by needed constituency).
- Dedicated constituency—no network survives without a dedicated constituency.

C.3. Site Identification and Selection

- Spanning gradients in climate or biomes with transects.
- Issues regarding representative spatial scale—site uniformity versus site clustering.
- Alignment with and contribution to network mission.
- Exposure—ability to measure representative quantities.
- Logistics—ability to service station (Always or only in favorable weather?).
- Site redundancy (positive for quality control, negative for extra resources).
- Power—is AC needed?
- Site security—is protection from vandalism needed?
- Permitting often a major impediment and usually underestimated.

C.4. Station Hardware

- Survival—weather is the main cause of lost weather/climate data.
- Robustness of sensors—ability to measure and record in any condition.
- Quality—distrusted records are worthless and a waste of time and money.
  - High quality—will cost up front but pays off later.
  - Low quality—may provide a lower start-up cost but will cost more later (low cost can be expensive).
- Redundancy—backup if sensors malfunction.
- Ice and snow—measurements are much more difficult than rain measurements.
- Severe environments (expense is about two–three times greater than for stations in more benign settings).

C.5. Communications

- Reliability—live data have a much larger constituency.
- One-way or two-way.
  - Retrieval of missed transmissions.
  - Ability to reprogram data logger remotely.
  - Remote troubleshooting abilities.
  - Continuing versus one-time costs.
- Back-up procedures to prevent data loss during communication outages.
- Live communications increase problems but also increase value.

C.6. Maintenance

- Main reason why networks fail (and most networks do eventually fail!).
- <u>Key</u> issue with nearly every network.
- Who will perform maintenance?
- Degree of commitment and motivation to contribute.
- Periodic? On-demand as needed? Preventive?
- Equipment change-out schedules and upgrades for sensors and software.
- Automated stations require <u>skilled</u> and <u>experienced</u> labor.
- Calibration—sensors often drift (climate).
- Site maintenance essential (constant vegetation, surface conditions, nearby influences).
- Typical automated station will cost about $2K per year to maintain.
- Documentation—photos, notes, visits, changes, essential for posterity.
- Planning for equipment life cycle and technological advances.

C.7. Maintaining Programmatic Continuity and Corporate Knowledge

- Long-term vision and commitment needed.
- Institutionalizing versus personalizing—developing appropriate dependencies.

C.8. Data Flow

- Centralized ingest?
- Centralized access to data and data products?
- Local version available?
- Contract out work or do it yourself?
- Quality control of data.
- Archival.
- Metadata—historic information, not a snapshot. Every station should collect metadata.
- Post-collection processing, multiple data-ingestion paths.

C.9. Products

- Most basic product consists of the data values.
- Summaries.
- Write own applications or leverage existing mechanisms?

C.10. Funding

- Prototype approaches as proof of concept.
- Linking and leveraging essential.
- Constituencies—every network <u>needs</u> a constituency.
- Bridging to practical and operational communities? Live data needed.
- Bridging to counterpart research efforts and initiatives—funding source.
- Creativity, resourcefulness, and persistence usually are essential to success.

C.11. Final Comments

- Deployment is by far the easiest part in operating a network.
- Maintenance is the main issue.
- Best analogy: Operating a network is like raising a child; it requires constant attention.

Source: Western Regional Climate Center (WRCC)

Appendix D. General design considerations for weather/climate-monitoring programs

The process for designing a climate-monitoring program benefits from anticipating design and protocol issues discussed here. Much of this material is been excerpted from a report addressing the Channel Islands National Park (Redmond and McCurdy 2005), where an example is found illustrating how these factors can be applied to a specific setting. Many national park units possess some climate or meteorology feature that sets them apart from more familiar or "standard" settings.

D.1. Introduction

There are several criteria that must be used in deciding to deploy new stations and where these new stations should be sited.

- Where are existing stations located?
- Where have data been gathered in the past (discontinued locations)?
- Where would a new station fill a knowledge gap about basic, long-term climatic averages for an area of interest?
- Where would a new station fill a knowledge gap about how climate behaves over time?
- As a special case for behavior over time, what locations might be expected to show a more sensitive response to climate change?
- How do answers to the preceding questions depend on the climate element? Are answers the same for precipitation, temperature, wind, snowfall, humidity, etc.?
- What role should manual measurements play? How should manual measurements interface with automated measurements?
- Are there special technical or management issues, either present or anticipated in the next 5–15 years, requiring added climate information?
- What unique information is provided in addition to information from existing sites? "Redundancy is bad."
- What nearby information is available to estimate missing observations because observing systems always experience gaps and lose data? "Redundancy is good."
- How would logistics and maintenance affect these decisions?

In relation to the preceding questions, there are several topics that should be considered. The following topics are not listed in a particular order.

D.1.1. Network Purpose

Humans seem to have an almost reflexive need to measure temperature and precipitation, along with other climate elements. These reasons span a broad range from utilitarian to curiosity-driven. Although there are well-known recurrent patterns of need and data use, new uses are always appearing. The number of uses ranges in the thousands. Attempts have been made to categorize such uses (see NRC 1998; NRC 2001). Because climate measurements are accumulated over a long time, they should be treated as multi-purpose and should be undertaken in a manner that serves the widest possible applications. Some applications remain constant, while others rise and fall in importance. An insistent issue today may subside, while the next pressing issue of tomorrow barely may be anticipated. The notion that humans might affect the climate of the entire Earth was nearly unimaginable when the national USDA (later NOAA) cooperative weather network began in the late 1800s. Abundant experience has shown, however, that there always will be a demand for a history record of climate measurements and their properties. Experience also shows that there is an expectation that climate measurements will be taken and made available to the general public.

An exhaustive list of uses for data would fill many pages and still be incomplete. In broad terms, however, there are needs to document environmental conditions that disrupt or otherwise affect park operations (e.g., storms and droughts). Design and construction standards are determined by climatological event frequencies that exceed certain thresholds. Climate is a determinant that sometimes attracts and sometimes discourages visitors. Climate may play a large part in the park experience (e.g., Death Valley and heat are nearly synonymous). Some park units are large enough to encompass spatial or elevation diversity in climate and the sequence of events can vary considerably inside or close to park boundaries. That is, temporal trends and statistics may not be the same everywhere, and this spatial structure should be sampled. The granularity of this structure depends on the presence of topography or large climate gradients or both, such as that found along the U.S. West Coast in summer with the rapid transition from the marine layer to the hot interior.

Plant and animal communities and entire ecosystems react to every nuance in the physical environment. No aspect of weather and climate goes undetected in the natural world. Wilson (1998) proposed "an informal rule of biological evolution" that applies here: "If an organic sensor can be imagined that is capable of detecting any particular environmental signal, a species exists somewhere that possesses this sensor." Every weather and climate event, whether dull or extraordinary to humans, matters to some organism. Dramatic events and creeping incremental change both have consequences to living systems. Extreme events or disturbances can "reset the clock" or "shake up the system" and lead to reverberations that last for years to centuries or longer. Slow change can carry complex nonlinear systems (e.g., any living assemblage) into states where chaotic transitions and new behavior occur. These changes are seldom predictable, typically are observed after the fact, and understood only in retrospect. Climate changes may not be exciting, but as a well-known atmospheric scientist, Mike Wallace, from the University of Washington once noted, "subtle does not mean unimportant."

Thus, individuals who observe the climate should be able to record observations accurately and depict both rapid and slow changes. In particular, an array of artificial influences easily can confound detection of slow changes. The record as provided can contain both real climate variability (that took place in the atmosphere) and fake climate variability (that arose directly from the way atmospheric changes were observed and recorded). As an example, trees growing near a climate station with an excellent anemometer will make it appear that the wind gradually slowed down over many years. Great care must be taken to protect against sources of fake climate variability on the longer-time scales of years to decades. Processes leading to the observed climate are not stationary; rather these processes draw from probability distributions that vary with time. For this reason, climatic time series do not exhibit statistical stationarity. The implications are manifold. There are no true climatic "normals" to which climate inevitably must return. Rather, there are broad ranges of climatic conditions. Climate does not demonstrate exact repetition but instead continual fluctuation and sometimes approximate repetition. In addition, there is always new behavior waiting to occur. Consequently, the business of climate monitoring is never finished, and there is no point where we can state confidently that "enough" is known.

D.1.2. Robustness
The most frequent cause for loss of weather data is the weather itself, the very thing we wish to record. The design of climate and weather observing programs should consider the meteorological equivalent of "peaking power" employed by utilities. Because environmental disturbances have significant effects on ecologic systems, sensors, data loggers, and communications networks should be able to function during the most severe conditions that realistically can be anticipated over the next 50–100 years. Systems designed in this manner are less likely to fail under more ordinary conditions, as well as more likely to transmit continuous, quality data for both tranquil and active periods.

D.1.3. Weather versus Climate
For "weather" measurements, pertaining to what is approximately happening here and now, small moves and changes in exposure are not as critical. For "climate" measurements, where values from different points in time are compared, siting and exposure are critical factors, and it is vitally important that the observing circumstances remain essentially unchanged over the duration of the station record.

Station moves can affect different elements to differing degrees. Even small moves of several meters, especially vertically, can affect temperature records. Hills and knolls act differently from the bottoms of small swales, pockets, or drainage channels (Whiteman 2000; Geiger et al. 2003). Precipitation is probably less subject to change with moves of 50–100 m than other elements (that is, precipitation has less intrinsic variation in small spaces) except if wind flow over the gauge is affected.

D.1.4. Physical Setting
Siting and exposure, and their continuity and consistency through time, significantly influence the climate records produced by a station. These two terms have overlapping connotations. We use the term "siting" in a more general sense, reserving the term "exposure" generally for the particular circumstances affecting the ability of an instrument to record measurements that are representative of the desired spatial or temporal scale.

D.1.5. Measurement Intervals
Climatic processes occur continuously in time, but our measurement systems usually record in discrete chunks of time: for example, seconds, hours, or days. These measurements often are referred to as "systematic" measurements. Interval averages may hide active or interesting periods of highly intense activity. Alternatively, some systems record "events" when a certain threshold of activity is exceeded (examples: another millimeter of precipitation has fallen, another kilometer of wind has moved past, the temperature has changed by a degree, a gust higher than 9.9 m/s has been measured). When this occurs, measurements from all sensors are reported. These measurements are known as "breakpoint" data. In relatively unchanging conditions (long calm periods or rainless weeks, for example), event recorders should send a signal that they are still "alive and well." If systematic recorders are programmed to note and periodically report the highest, lowest, and mean value within each time interval, the likelihood

is reduced that interesting behavior will be glossed over or lost. With the capacity of modern data loggers, it is recommended to record and report extremes within the basic time increment (e.g., hourly or 10 minutes). This approach also assists quality-control procedures.

There is usually a trade-off between data volume and time increment, and most automated systems now are set to record approximately hourly. A number of field stations maintained by WRCC are programmed to record in 5- or 10-minute increments, which readily serve to construct an hourly value. However, this approach produces 6–12 times as much data as hourly data. These systems typically do not record details of events at sub-interval time scales, but they easily can record peak values, or counts of threshold exceedance, within the time intervals.

Thus, for each time interval at an automated station, we recommend that several kinds of information—mean or sum, extreme maximum and minimum, and sometimes standard deviation—be recorded. These measurements are useful for quality control and other purposes. Modern data loggers and office computers have quite high capacity. Diagnostic information indicating the state of solar chargers or battery voltages and their extremes is of great value. This topic will be discussed in greater detail in a succeeding section.

Automation also has made possible adaptive or intelligent monitoring techniques where systems vary the recording rate based on detection of the behavior of interest by the software. Sub-interval behavior of interest can be masked on occasion (e.g., a 5-minute extreme downpour with high-erosive capability hidden by an innocuous hourly total). Most users prefer measurements that are systematic in time because they are much easier to summarize and manipulate.

For breakpoint data produced by event reporters, there also is a need to send periodically a signal that the station is still functioning, even though there is nothing more to report. "No report" does not necessarily mean "no data," and it is important to distinguish between the actual observation that was recorded and the content of that observation (e.g., an observation of "0.00" is not the same as "no observation").

D.1.6. Mixed Time Scales
There are times when we may wish to combine information from radically different scales. For example, over the past 100 years we may want to know how the frequency of 5-minute precipitation peaks has varied or how the frequency of peak 1-second wind gusts have varied. We may also want to know over this time if nearby vegetation gradually has grown up to increasingly block the wind or to slowly improve precipitation catch. Answers to these questions require knowledge over a wide range of time scales.

D.1.7. Elements
For manual measurements, the typical elements recorded included temperature extremes, precipitation, and snowfall/snow depth. Automated measurements typically include temperature, precipitation, humidity, wind speed and direction, and solar radiation. An exception to this exists in very windy locations where precipitation is difficult to measure accurately. Automated measurements of snow are improving, but manual measurements are still preferable, as long as shielding is present. Automated measurement of frozen precipitation presents numerous challenges that have not been resolved fully, and the best gauges are quite expensive ($3–8K).

Soil temperatures also are included sometimes. Soil moisture is extremely useful, but measurements are not made at many sites. In addition, care must be taken in the installation and maintenance of instruments used in measuring soil moisture. Soil properties vary tremendously in short distances as well, and it is often very difficult ("impossible") to accurately document these variations (without digging up all the soil!). In cooler climates, ultrasonic sensors that detect snow depth are becoming commonplace.

D.1.8. Wind Standards

Wind varies the most in the shortest distance, since it always decreases to zero near the ground and increases rapidly (approximately logarithmically) with height near the ground. Changes in anemometer height obviously will affect distribution of wind speed as will changes in vegetation, obstructions such as buildings, etc. A site that has a 3-m (10-ft) mast clearly will be less windy than a site that has a 6-m (20-ft) or 10-m (33-ft) mast. Historically, many U.S. airports (FAA and NWS) and most current RAWS sites have used a standard 6-m (20-ft) mast for wind measurements. Some NPS RAWS sites utilize shorter masts. Over the last decade, as Automated Surface Observing Systems (ASOSs, mostly NWS) and Automated Weather Observing Systems (AWOSs, mostly FAA) have been deployed at most airports, wind masts have been raised to 8 or 10 m (26 or 33 ft), depending on airplane clearance. The World Meteorological Organization recommends 10 m as the height for wind measurements (WMO 1983; 2005), and more groups are migrating slowly to this standard. The American Association of State Climatologists (AASC 1985) have recommended that wind be measured at 3 m, a standard geared more for agricultural applications than for general purpose uses where higher levels usually are preferred. Different anemometers have different starting thresholds; therefore, areas that frequently experience very light winds may not produce wind measurements thus affecting long-term mean estimates of wind speed. For both sustained winds (averages over a short interval of 2–60 minutes) and especially for gusts, the duration of the sampling interval makes a considerable difference. For the same wind history, 1–second gusts are higher than gusts averaging 3 seconds, which in turn are greater than 5-second averages, so that the same sequence would be described with different numbers (all three systems and more are in use). Changes in the averaging procedure, or in height or exposure, can lead to "false" or "fake" climate change with no change in actual climate. Changes in any of these should be noted in the metadata.

D.1.9. Wind Nomenclature

Wind is a vector quantity having a direction and a speed. Directions can be two- or three-dimensional; they will be three-dimensional if the vertical component is important. In all common uses, winds always are denoted by the direction they blow *from* (north wind or southerly breeze). This convention exists because wind often brings weather, and thus our attention is focused upstream. However, this approach contrasts with the way ocean currents are viewed. Ocean currents usually are denoted by the direction they are moving *towards* (eastward current moves from west to east). In specialized applications (such as in atmospheric modeling), wind velocity vectors point in the direction that the wind is blowing. Thus, a southwesterly wind (from the southwest) has both northward and eastward (to the north and to the east) components. Except near mountains, wind cannot blow up or down near the ground, so the vertical component of wind often is approximated as zero, and the horizontal component is emphasized.

D.1.10. Frozen Precipitation

Frozen precipitation is more difficult to measure than liquid precipitation, especially with automated techniques. Sevruk and Harmon (1984), Goodison et al. (1998), and Yang et al. (1998; 2001) provide many of the reasons to explain this. The importance of frozen precipitation varies greatly from one setting to another. This subject was discussed in greater detail in a related inventory and monitoring report for the Alaska park units (Redmond et al. 2005).

In climates that receive frozen precipitation, a decision must be made whether or not to try to record such events accurately. This usually means that the precipitation must be turned into liquid either by falling into an antifreeze fluid solution that is then weighed or by heating the precipitation enough to melt and fall through a measuring mechanism such as a nearly-balanced tipping bucket. Accurate measurements from the first approach require expensive gauges; tipping buckets can achieve this resolution readily but are more apt to lose some or all precipitation. Improvements have been made to the heating mechanism on the NWS tipping-bucket gauge used for the ASOS to correct its numerous deficiencies making it less problematic; however, this gauge is not inexpensive. A heat supply needed to melt frozen precipitation usually requires more energy than renewable energy (solar panels or wind recharging) can provide thus AC power is needed. Periods of frozen precipitation or rime often provide less-than-optimal recharging conditions with heavy clouds, short days, low-solar-elevation angles and more horizon blocking, and cold temperatures causing additional drain on the battery.

D.1.11. Save or Lose

A second consideration with precipitation is determining if the measurement should be saved (as in weighing systems) or lost (as in tipping-bucket systems). With tipping buckets, after the water has passed through the tipping mechanism, it usually just drops to the ground. Thus, there is no checksum to ensure that the sum of all the tips adds up to what has been saved in a reservoir at some location. By contrast, the weighing gauges continually accumulate until the reservoir is emptied, the reported value is the total reservoir content (for example, the height of the liquid column in a tube), and the incremental precipitation is the difference in depth between two known times. These weighing gauges do not always have the same fine resolution. Some gauges only record to the nearest centimeter, which is usually acceptable for hydrology but not necessarily for other needs. (For reference, a millimeter of precipitation can get a person in street clothes quite wet.) Other weighing gauges are capable of measuring to the 0.25-mm (0.01-in.) resolution but do not have as much capacity and must be emptied more often. Day/night and storm-related thermal expansion and contraction and sometimes wind shaking can cause fluid pressure from accumulated totals to go up and down in SNOTEL gauges by small increments (commonly 0.3-3 cm, or 0.01–0.10 ft) leading to "negative precipitation" followed by similarly non-real light precipitation when, in fact, no change took place in the amount of accumulated precipitation.

D.1.12. Time

Time should always be in local standard time (LST), and daylight savings time (DST) should never be used under any circumstances with automated equipment and timers. Using DST leads to one duplicate hour, one missing hour, and a season of displaced values, as well as needless confusion and a data-management nightmare. Absolute time, such as Greenwich Mean Time (GMT) or Coordinated Universal Time (UTC), also can be used because these formats are unambiguously translatable. Since measurements only provide information about what already *has* occurred or *is* occurring and not what *will* occur, they should always be assigned to the *ending time* of the associated interval with hour 24 marking the end of the last hour of the day. In this system, midnight always represents the end of the day, not the start. To demonstrate the importance of this differentiation, we have encountered situations where police officers seeking corroborating weather data could not recall whether the time on their crime report from a year ago was the starting midnight or the ending midnight! Station positions should be known to within a few meters, easily accomplished with GPS, so that time zones and solar angles can be determined accurately.

D.1.13. Automated versus Manual

Most of this report has addressed automated measurements. Historically, most measurements are manual and typically collected once a day. In many cases, manual measurements continue because of habit, usefulness, and desire for continuity over time. Manual measurements are extremely useful and when possible should be encouraged. However, automated measurements are becoming more common. For either, it is important to record time in a logically consistent manner.

It should not be automatically assumed that newer data and measurements are "better" than older data or that manual data are "worse" than automated data. Older or simpler manual measurements are often of very high quality even if they sometimes are not in the most convenient digital format.

There is widespread desire to use automated systems to reduce human involvement. This is admirable and understandable, but every automated weather/climate station or network requires significant human attention and maintenance. A telling example concerns the Oklahoma Mesonet (see Brock et al. 1995, and bibliography at http://www.mesonet.ou.edu), a network of about 115 high–quality, automated meteorological stations spread over Oklahoma, where about 80 percent of the annual ($2–3M) budget is nonetheless allocated to humans with only about 20 percent allocated to equipment.

D.1.14. Manual Conventions

Manual measurements typically are made once a day. Elements usually consist of maximum and minimum temperature, temperature at observation time, precipitation, snowfall, snow depth, and sometimes evaporation, wind, or other information. Since it is not actually known when extremes occurred, the only logical approach, and the nationwide convention, is to ascribe the entire measurement to the time-interval date and to enter it on the form in that way. For morning observers (for example, 8 am to 8 am), this means that the maximum temperature written for today often is from yesterday afternoon and sometimes the minimum temperature for the 24-hr period actually occurred yesterday morning. However, this is understood and expected. It is often a surprise to observers to see how many maximum temperatures do not occur in the afternoon and how many minimum temperatures do not occur in the predawn hours. This is especially true in environments that are colder, higher, northerly, cloudy, mountainous, or coastal. As long as this convention is strictly followed every day, it has been shown that truly excellent climate records can result (Redmond 1992). Manual observers should reset equipment only one time per day at the official observing time. Making more than one measurement a day is discouraged strongly; this practice results in a hybrid record that is too difficult to interpret. The only exception is for total daily snowfall. New snowfall can be measured up to four times per day with no observations closer than six hours. It is well known that more frequent measurement of snow increases the annual total because compaction is a continuous process.

Two main purposes for climate observations are to establish the long-term averages for given locations and to track variations in climate. Broadly speaking, these purposes address topics of absolute and relative climate behavior. Once absolute behavior has been "established" (a task that is never finished because long-term averages continue to vary in time)—temporal variability quickly becomes the item of most interest.

D.2. Representativeness

Having discussed important factors to consider when new sites are installed, we now turn our attention to site "representativeness." In popular usage, we often encounter the notion that a site is "representative" of another site if it receives the same annual precipitation or records the same annual temperature or if some other element-specific, long-term average has a similar value. This notion of representativeness has a certain limited validity, but there are other aspects of this idea that need to be considered.

A climate monitoring site also can be said to be representative if climate records from that site show sufficiently strong temporal correlations with a large number of locations over a sufficiently large area. If station A receives 20 cm a year and station B receives 200 cm a year, these climates obviously receive quite differing amounts of precipitation. However, if their monthly, seasonal, or annual correlations are high (for example, 0.80 or higher for a particular time scale), one site can be used as a surrogate for estimating values at the other if measurements for a particular month, season, or year are missing. That is, a wet or dry month at one station is also a wet or dry month (relative to its own mean) at the comparison station. Note that high correlations on one time scale do not imply automatically that high correlations will occur on other time scales.

Likewise, two stations having similar mean climates (for example, similar annual precipitation) might not co-vary in close synchrony (for example, coastal versus interior). This may be considered a matter of climate "affiliation" for a particular location.

Thus, the representativeness of a site can refer either to the basic climatic averages for a given duration (or time window within the annual cycle) or to the extent that the site co-varies in time with respect to all surrounding locations. One site can be representative of another in the first sense but not the second, or vice versa, or neither, or both—all combinations are possible.

If two sites are perfectly correlated then, in a sense, they are "redundant." However, redundancy has value because all sites will experience missing data especially with automated equipment in rugged environments and harsh climates where outages and other problems nearly can be guaranteed. In many cases, those outages are caused by the weather, particularly by unusual weather and the very conditions we most wish to know about. Methods for filling in those values will require proxy information from this or other nearby networks. Thus, redundancy is a virtue rather than a vice.

In general, the cooperative stations managed by the NWS have produced much longer records than automated stations like RAWS or SNOTEL stations. The RAWS stations often have problems with precipitation, especially in winter, or with missing data, so that low correlations may be data problems rather than climatic dissimilarity. The RAWS records also are relatively short, so correlations should be interpreted with care. In performing and interpreting such analyses, however, we must remember that there are physical climate reasons and observational reasons why stations within a short distance (even a few tens or hundreds of meters) may not correlate well.

D.2.1. Temporal Behavior

It is possible that high correlations will occur between station pairs during certain portions of the year (i.e., January) but low correlations may occur during other portions of the year (e.g., September or October). The relative contributions of these seasons to the annual total (for precipitation) or average (for temperature) and the correlations for each month are both factors in the correlation of an aggregated time window of longer duration that encompasses those seasons (e.g., one of the year definitions such as calendar year or water year). A complete and careful evaluation ideally would include such a correlation analysis but requires more resources and data. Note that it also is possible and frequently is observed that temperatures are highly correlated while precipitation is not or vice versa, and these relations can change according to the time of year. If two stations are well correlated for all climate elements for all portions of the year, then they can be considered redundant.

With scarce resources, the initial strategy should be to try to identify locations that do not correlate particularly well, so that each new site measures something new that cannot be guessed easily from the behavior of surrounding sites. (An important caveat here is that lack of such correlation could be a result of physical climate behavior and not a result of faults with the actual measuring process; i.e., by unrepresentative or simply poor-quality data. Unfortunately, we seldom have perfect climate data.) As additional sites are added, we usually wish for some combination of unique and redundant sites to meet what amounts to essentially orthogonal constraints: new information and more reliably-furnished information.

A common consideration is whether to observe on a ridge or in a valley, given the resources to place a single station within a particular area of a few square kilometers. Ridge and valley stations will correlate very well for temperatures when lapse conditions prevail, particularly summer daytime temperatures. In summer at night or winter at daylight, the picture will be more mixed and correlations will be lower. In winter at night when inversions are common and even the rule, correlations may be zero or even negative and perhaps even more divergent as the two sites are on opposite sides of the inversion. If we had the luxury of locating stations everywhere, we would find that ridge tops generally correlate very well with other ridge tops and similarly valleys with other valleys, but ridge tops correlate well with valleys only under certain circumstances. Beyond this, valleys and ridges having similar orientations usually will correlate better with each other than those with perpendicular orientations, depending on their orientation with respect to large-scale wind flow and solar angles.

Unfortunately, we do not have stations everywhere, so we are forced to use the few comparisons that we have and include a large dose of intelligent reasoning, using what we have observed elsewhere. In performing and interpreting such analyses, we must remember that there are physical climatic reasons and observational reasons why stations within a short distance (even a few tens or hundreds of meters) may not correlate well.

Examples of correlation analyses include those for the Channel Islands and for southwest Alaska, which can be found in Redmond and McCurdy (2005) and Redmond et al. (2005). These examples illustrate what can be learned from correlation analyses. Spatial correlations generally vary by time of year. Thus, results should be displayed in the form of annual correlation cycles— for monthly mean temperature and monthly total precipitation and perhaps other climate elements like wind or humidity—between station pairs selected for climatic setting and data availability and quality.

In general, the COOP stations managed by the NWS have produced much longer records than have automated stations like RAWS or SNOTEL stations. The RAWS stations also often have problems with precipitation, especially in winter or with missing data, so that low correlations may be data problems rather than climate dissimilarity. The RAWS records are much shorter, so correlations should be interpreted with care, but these stations are more likely to be in places of interest for remote or under-sampled regions.

D.2.2. Spatial Behavior
A number of techniques exist to interpolate from isolated point values to a spatial domain. For example, a common technique is simple inverse distance weighting. Critical to the success of the simplest of such techniques is that some other property of the spatial domain, one that is influential for the mapped element, does not vary significantly. Topography greatly influences precipitation, temperature, wind, humidity, and most other meteorological elements. Thus, this criterion clearly is not met in any region having extreme topographic diversity. In such circumstances, simple Cartesian distance may have little to do with how rapidly correlation deteriorates from one site to the next, and in fact, the correlations can decrease readily from a mountain to a valley and then increase again on the next mountain. Such structure in the fields of spatial correlation is not seen in the relatively (statistically) well-behaved flat areas like those in the eastern U.S.

To account for dominating effects such as topography and inland–coastal differences that exist in certain regions, some kind of additional knowledge must be brought to bear to produce meaningful, physically plausible, and observationally based interpolations. Historically, this has proven to be an extremely difficult problem, especially to perform objective and repeatable analyses. An analysis performed for southwest Alaska (Redmond et al. 2005) concluded that the PRISM maps (Daly et al. 1994; 2002; Gibson et al. 2002; Doggett et al. 2004) were probably the best available. An analysis by Simpson et al. (2005) further discussed many issues in the mapping of Alaska's climate and resulted in the same conclusion about PRISM.

D.2.3. Climate-Change Detection
Although general purpose climate stations should be situated to address all aspects of climate variability, it is desirable that they also be in locations that are more sensitive to climate change

from natural or anthropogenic influences should it begin to occur. The question here is how well we know such sensitivities. The climate-change issue is quite complex because it encompasses more than just greenhouse gasses.

Sites that are in locations or climates particularly vulnerable to climate change should be favored. How this vulnerability is determined is a considerably challenging research issue. Candidate locations or situations are those that lie on the border between two major biomes or just inside the edge of one or the other. In these cases, a slight movement of the boundary in anticipated direction (toward "warmer," for example) would be much easier to detect as the boundary moves past the site and a different set of biota begin to be established. Such a vegetative or ecologic response would be more visible and would take less time to establish as a real change than would a smaller change in the center of the distribution range of a marker or key species.

D.2.4. Element-Specific Differences
The various climate elements (temperature, precipitation, cloudiness, snowfall, humidity, wind speed and direction, solar radiation) do not vary through time in the same sequence or manner nor should they necessarily be expected to vary in this manner. The spatial patterns of variability should not be expected to be the same for all elements. These patterns also should not be expected to be similar for all months or seasons. The suitability of individual sites for measurement also varies from one element to another. A site that has a favorable exposure for temperature or wind may not have a favorable exposure for precipitation or snowfall. A site that experiences proper air movement may be situated in a topographic channel, such as a river valley or a pass, which restricts the range of wind directions and affects the distribution of speed-direction categories.

D.2.5. Logistics and Practical Factors
Even with the most advanced scientific rationale, sites in some remote or climatically challenging settings may not be suitable because of the difficulty in servicing and maintaining equipment. Contributing to these challenges are scheduling difficulties, animal behavior, snow burial, icing, snow behavior, access and logistical problems, and the weather itself. Remote and elevated sites usually require far more attention and expense than a rain-dominated, easily accessible valley location.

For climate purposes, station exposure and the local environment should be maintained in their original state (vegetation especially), so that changes seen are the result of regional climate variations and not of trees growing up, bushes crowding a site, surface albedo changing, fire clearing, etc. Repeat photography has shown many examples of slow environmental change in the vicinity of a station in rather short time frames (5–20 years), and this technique should be employed routinely and frequently at all locations. In the end, logistics, maintenance, and other practical factors almost always determine the success of weather- and climate-monitoring activities.

D.2.6. Personnel Factors
Many past experiences (almost exclusively negative) strongly support the necessity to place primary responsibility for station deployment and maintenance in the hands of seasoned, highly

qualified, trained, and meticulously careful personnel, the more experienced the better. Over time, even in "benign" climates but especially where harsher conditions prevail, every conceivable problem will occur and both the usual and unusual should be anticipated: weather, animals, plants, salt, sensor and communication failure, windblown debris, corrosion, power failures, vibrations, avalanches, snow loading and creep, corruption of the data logger program, etc. An ability to anticipate and forestall such problems, a knack for innovation and improvisation, knowledge of electronics, practical and organizational skills, and presence of mind to bring the various small but vital parts, spares, tools, and diagnostic troubleshooting equipment are highly valued qualities. Especially when logistics are so expensive, a premium should be placed on using experienced personnel, since the slightest and seemingly most minor mistake can render a station useless or, even worse, uncertain. Exclusive reliance on individuals without this background can be costly and almost always will result eventually in unnecessary loss of data. Skilled labor and an apprenticeship system to develop new skilled labor will greatly reduce (but not eliminate) the types of problems that can occur in operating a climate network.

D.3. Site Selection

In addition to considerations identified previously in this appendix, various factors need to be considered in selecting sites for new or augmented instrumentation.

D.3.1. Equipment and Exposure Factors

D.3.1.1. Measurement Suite: All sites should measure temperature, humidity, wind, solar radiation, and snow depth. Precipitation measurements are more difficult but probably should be attempted with the understanding that winter measurements may be of limited or no value unless an all-weather gauge has been installed. Even if an all-weather gauge has been installed, it is desirable to have a second gauge present that operates on a different principle–for example, a fluid-based system like those used in the SNOTEL stations in tandem with a higher–resolution, tipping bucket gauge for summertime. Without heating, a tipping bucket gauge usually is of use only when temperatures are above freezing and when temperatures have not been below freezing for some time, so that accumulated ice and snow is not melting and being recorded as present precipitation. Gauge undercatch is a significant issue in snowy climates, so shielding should be considered for all gauges designed to work over the winter months. It is very important to note the presence or absence of shielding, the type of shielding, and the dates of installation or removal of the shielding.

D.3.1.2. Overall Exposure: The ideal, general all-purpose site has gentle slopes, is open to the sun and the wind, has a natural vegetative cover, avoids strong local (less than 200 m) influences, and represents a reasonable compromise among all climate elements. The best temperature sites are not the best precipitation sites, and the same is true for other elements. Steep topography in the immediate vicinity should be avoided unless settings where precipitation is affected by steep topography are being deliberately sought or a mountaintop or ridgeline is the desired location. The potential for disturbance should be considered: fire and flood risk, earth movement, wind-borne debris, volcanic deposits or lahars, vandalism, animal tampering, and general human encroachment are all factors.

D.3.1.3. Elevation: Mountain climates do not vary in time in exactly the same manner as adjoining valley climates. This concept is emphasized when temperature inversions are present to a greater degree and during precipitation when winds rise up the slopes at the same angle. There is considerable concern that mountain climates will be (or already are) changing and perhaps changing differently than lowland climates, which has direct and indirect consequences for plant and animal life in the more extreme zones. Elevations of special significance are those that are near the mean rain/snow line for winter, near the tree line, and near the mean annual freezing level (all of these may not be quite the same). Because the lapse rates in wet climates often are nearly moist-adiabatic during the main precipitation seasons, measurements at one elevation may be extrapolated to nearby elevations. In drier climates and in the winter, temperature and to a lesser extent wind will show various elevation profiles.

D.3.1.4. Transects: The concept of observing transects that span climatic gradients is sound. This is not always straightforward in topographically uneven terrain, but these transects could still be arranged by setting up station(s) along the coast; in or near passes atop the main coastal interior drainage divide; and inland at one, two, or three distances into the interior lowlands. Transects need not—and by dint of topographic constraints probably cannot—be straight lines, but the closer that a line can be approximated the better. The main point is to systematically sample the key points of a behavioral transition without deviating too radically from linearity.

D.3.1.5. Other Topographic Considerations: There are various considerations with respect to local topography. Local topography can influence wind (channeling, upslope/downslope, etc.), precipitation (orographic enhancement, downslope evaporation, catch efficiency, etc.), and temperature (frost pockets, hilltops, aspect, mixing or decoupling from the overlying atmosphere, bowls, radiative effects, etc.), to different degrees at differing scales. In general, for measurements to be areally representative, it is better to avoid these local effects to the extent that they can be identified before station deployment (once deployed, it is desirable not to move a station). The primary purpose of a climate-monitoring network should be to serve as an infrastructure in the form of a set of benchmark stations for comparing other stations. Sometimes, however, it is exactly these local phenomena that we want to capture. Living organisms, especially plants, are affected by their immediate environment, whether it is representative of a larger setting or not. Specific measurements of limited scope and duration made for these purposes then can be tied to the main benchmarks. This experience is useful also in determining the complexity needed in the benchmark monitoring process in order to capture particular phenomena at particular space and time scales.

Sites that drain (cold air) well generally are better than sites that allow cold air to pool. Slightly sloped areas (1 degree is fine) or small benches from tens to hundreds of meters above streams are often favorable locations. Furthermore, these sites often tend to be out of the path of hazards (like floods) and to have rocky outcroppings where controlling vegetation will not be a major concern. Benches or wide spots on the rise between two forks of a river system are often the only flat areas and sometimes jut out to give greater exposure to winds from more directions.

D.3.1.6. Prior History: The starting point in designing a program is to determine what kinds of observations have been collected over time, by whom, in what manner, and if these observation are continuing to the present time. It also may be of value to "re-occupy" the former site of a station that is now inactive to provide some measure of continuity or a reference point from the past. This can be of value even if continuous observations were not made during the entire intervening period.

D.3.2. Element-Specific Factors

D.3.2.1. Temperature: An open exposure with uninhibited air movement is the preferred setting. The most common measurement is made at approximately eye level, 1.5–2.0 m. In snowy locations sensors should be at least one meter higher than the deepest snowpack expected in the next 50 years or perhaps 2–3 times the depth of the average maximum annual depth. Sensors should be shielded above and below from solar radiation (bouncing off snow), from sunrise/sunset horizontal input, and from vertical rock faces. Sensors should be clamped tightly, so that they do not swivel away from level stacks of radiation plates. Nearby vegetation should be kept away from the sensors (several meters). Growing vegetation should be cut to original conditions. Small hollows and swales can cool tremendously at night, and it is best avoid these areas. Side slopes of perhaps a degree or two of angle facilitate air movement and drainage and, in effect, sample a large area during nighttime hours. The very bottom of a valley should be avoided. Temperature can change substantially from moves of only a few meters. Situations have been observed where flat and seemingly uniform conditions (like airport runways) appear to demonstrate different climate behaviors over short distances of a few tens or hundreds of meters (differences of 5–10°C). When snow is on the ground, these microclimatic differences can be stronger, and differences of 2–5°C can occur in the short distance between the thermometer and the snow surface on calm evenings.

D.3.2.2. Precipitation (liquid): Calm locations with vegetative or artificial shielding are preferred. Wind will adversely impact readings; therefore, the less the better. Wind effects on precipitation are far less for rain than for snow. Devices that "save" precipitation present advantages, but most gauges are built to dump precipitation as it falls or to empty periodically. Automated gauges give both the amount and the timing. Simple backups that record only the total precipitation since the last visit have a certain advantage (for example, storage gauges or lengths of PVC pipe perhaps with bladders on the bottom). The following question should be asked: Does the total precipitation from an automated gauge add up to the measured total in a simple bucket (evaporation is prevented with an appropriate substance such as mineral oil)? Drip from overhanging foliage and trees can augment precipitation totals.

D.3.2.3. Precipitation (frozen): Calm locations or shielding are a must. Undercatch for rain is only about 5 percent, but with winds of only 2–4 m/s, gauges may catch only 30–70 percent of the actual snow falling depending on density of the flakes. To catch 100 percent of the snow, the standard configuration for shielding is employed by the CRN (Climate Reference Network): the DFIR (Double-Fence Intercomparison Reference) shield with 2.4-m (8-ft.) vertical, wooden slatted fences in two concentric octagons with diameters of 8 m and 4 m (26 ft and 13 ft, respectively) and an inner Alter shield (flapping vanes). Numerous tests have shown this is the only way to achieve complete catch of snowfall (e.g., Yang et al. 1998, 2001). The DFIR shield is large and bulky; it is recommended that all precipitation gauges have at least Alter shields on them.

Near oceans, much snow is heavy and falls more vertically. In colder locations or storms, light flakes frequently will fly in and then out of the gauge. Clearings in forests are usually excellent sites. Snow blowing from trees that are too close can augment actual precipitation totals. Artificial shielding (vanes, etc.) placed around gauges in snowy locales always should be used if accurate totals are desired. Moving parts tend to freeze up. Capping of gauges during heavy snowfall events is a common occurrence. When the cap becomes pointed, snow falls off to the ground and is not recorded. Caps and plugs often will not fall into the tube until hours, days, or even weeks have passed, typically during an extended period of freezing temperature or above or when sunlight finally occurs. Liquid-based measurements (e.g., SNOTEL "rocket" gauges) do not have the resolution (usually 0.3 cm [0.1 in.] rather than 0.03 cm [0.01 in.]) that tipping bucket and other gauges have but are known to be reasonably accurate in very snowy climates. Light snowfall events might not be recorded until enough of them add up to the next reporting increment. More expensive gauges like Geonors can be considered and could do quite well in snowy settings; however, they need to be emptied every 40 cm (15 in.) or so (capacity of 51 cm [20 in.]) until the new 91-cm (36-in.) capacity gauge is offered for sale. Recently, the NWS has been trying out the new (and very expensive) Ott all-weather gauge. Riming can be an issue in windy foggy environments below freezing. Rime, dew, and other forms of atmospheric condensation are not real precipitation, since they are caused by the gauge.

D.3.2.4. Snow Depth: Windswept areas tend to be blown clear of snow. Conversely, certain types of vegetation can act as a snow fence and cause artificial drifts. However, some amount of vegetation in the vicinity generally can help slow down the wind. The two most common types of snow-depth gauges are the Judd Snow Depth Sensor, produced by Judd Communications, and the snow depth gauge produced by Campbell Scientific, Inc. Opinions vary on which one is better. These gauges use ultrasound and look downward in a cone about 22 degrees in diameter. The ground should be relatively clear of vegetation and maintained in a manner so that the zero point on the calibration scale does not change.

D.3.2.5. Snow Water Equivalent: This is determined by the weight of snow on fluid-filled pads about the size of a desktop set up sometimes in groups of four or in larger hexagons several meters in diameter. These pads require flat ground some distance from nearby sources of windblown snow and shielding that is "just right": not too close to the shielding to act as a kind of snow fence and not too far from the shielding so that blowing and drifting become a factor. Generally, these pads require fluids that possess antifreeze-like properties, as well as handling and replacement protocols.

D.3.2.6. Wind: Open exposures are needed for wind measurements. Small prominences or benches without blockage from certain sectors are preferred. A typical rule for trees is to site stations back 10 tree-heights from all tree obstructions. Sites in long, narrow valleys can obviously only exhibit two main wind directions. Gently rounded eminences are more favored. Any kind of topographic steering should be avoided to the extent possible. Avoiding major mountain chains or single isolated mountains or ridges is usually a favorable approach, if there is a choice. Sustained wind speed and the highest gusts (1-second) should be recorded. Averaging methodologies for both sustained winds and gusts can affect climate trends and should be recorded as metadata with all changes noted. Vegetation growth affects the vertical wind profile, and growth over a few years can lead to changes in mean wind speed even if the "real" wind does not change, so vegetation near the site (perhaps out to 50 m) should be maintained in a quasi-permanent status (same height and spatial distribution). Wind devices can rime up and freeze or spin out of balance. In severely rimed or windy climates, rugged anemometers, such as those made by Taylor, are worth considering. These anemometers are expensive but durable and can withstand substantial abuse. In exposed locations, personnel should plan for winds to be at least 50 m/s and be able to measure these wind speeds. At a minimum, anemometers should be rated to 75 m/s.

D.3.2.7. Humidity: Humidity is a relatively straightforward climate element. Close proximity to lakes or other water features can affect readings. Humidity readings typically are less accurate near 100 percent and at low humidities in cold weather.

D.3.2.8. Solar Radiation: A site with an unobstructed horizon obviously is the most desirable. This generally implies a flat plateau or summit. However, in most locations trees or mountains will obstruct the sun for part of the day.

D.3.2.9. Soil Temperature: It is desirable to measure soil temperature at locations where soil is present. If soil temperature is recorded at only a single depth, the most preferred depth is 10 cm. Other common depths include 25 cm, 50 cm, 2 cm, and 100 cm. Biological activity in the soil will be proportional to temperature with important threshold effects occurring near freezing.

D.3.2.10. Soil Moisture: Soil-moisture gauges are somewhat temperamental and require care to install. The soil should be characterized by a soil expert during installation of the gauge. The readings may require a certain level of experience to interpret correctly. If accurate, readings of soil moisture are especially useful.

D.3.2.11. Distributed Observations: It can be seen readily that compromises must be struck among the considerations described in the preceding paragraphs because some are mutually exclusive.

How large can a "site" be? Generally, the equipment footprint should be kept as small as practical with all components placed next to each other (within less than 10–20 m or so). Readings from one instrument frequently are used to aid in interpreting readings from the remaining instruments.

What is a tolerable degree of separation? Some consideration may be given to locating a precipitation gauge or snow pillow among protective vegetation, while the associated temperature, wind, and humidity readings would be collected more effectively in an open and exposed location within 20–50 m. Ideally, it is advantageous to know the wind measurement precisely at the precipitation gauge, but a compromise involving a short split, and in effect a "distributed observation," could be considered. There are no definitive rules governing this decision, but it is suggested that the site footprint be kept within approximately 50 m. There also are constraints imposed by engineering and electrical factors that affect cable lengths, signal strength, and line noise; therefore, the shorter the cable the better. Practical issues include the need to trench a channel to outlying instruments or to allow lines to lie atop the ground and associated problems with animals, humans, weathering, etc. Separating a precipitation gauge up to 100 m or so from an instrument mast may be an acceptable compromise if other factors are not limiting.

D.3.2.12. Instrument Replacement Schedules: Instruments slowly degrade, and a plan for replacing them with new, refurbished, or recalibrated instruments should be in place. After approximately five years, a systematic change-out procedure should result in replacing most sensors in a network. Certain parts, such as solar radiation sensors, are candidates for annual calibration or change-out. Anemometers tend to degrade as bearings erode or electrical contacts become uneven. Noisy bearings are an indication, and a stethoscope might aid in hearing such noises. Increased internal friction affects the threshold starting speed; once spinning, they tend to function properly. Increases in starting threshold speeds can lead to more zero-wind measurements and thus reduce the reported mean wind speed with no real change in wind properties. A field calibration kit should be developed and taken on all site visits, routine or otherwise. Rain gauges can be tested with drip testers during field visits. Protective conduit and tight water seals can prevent abrasion and moisture problems with the equipment, although seals can keep moisture in as well as out. Bulletproof casings sometimes are employed in remote settings. A supply of spare parts, at least one of each and more for less-expensive or more-delicate sensors, should be maintained to allow replacement of worn or nonfunctional instruments during field visits. In addition, this approach allows instruments to be calibrated in the relative convenience of the operational home—the larger the network, the greater the need for a parts depot.

D.3.3. Long-Term Comparability and Consistency

D.3.3.1. Consistency: The emphasis here is to hold biases constant. Every site has biases, problems, and idiosyncrasies of one sort or another. The best rule to follow is simply to try to keep biases constant through time. Since the goal is to track climate through time, keeping sensors, methodologies, and exposure constant will ensure that only true climate change is being measured. This means leaving the site in its original state or performing maintenance to keep it that way. Once a site is installed, the goal should be to never move the site even by a few meters or to allow significant changes to occur within 100 m for the next several decades.

Sites in or near rock outcroppings likely will experience less vegetative disturbance or growth through the years and will not usually retain moisture, a factor that could speed corrosion. Sites that will remain locally similar for some time are usually preferable. However, in some cases the intent of a station might be to record the local climate effects of changes within a small-scale system (for example, glacier, recently burned area, or scene of some other disturbance) that is subject to a regional climate influence. In this example, the local changes might be much larger than the regional changes.

D.3.3.2. Metadata: Since the climate of every site is affected by features in the immediate vicinity, it is vital to record this information over time and to update the record repeatedly at each service visit. Distances, angles, heights of vegetation, fine-scale topography, condition of instruments, shielding discoloration, and other factors from within a meter to several kilometers should be noted. Systematic photography should be undertaken and updated at least once every one–two years.

Photographic documentation should be taken at each site in a standard manner and repeated every two–three years. Guidelines for methodology were developed by Redmond (2004) as a result of experience with the NOAA CRN and can be found on the WRCC NPS Web pages at http://www.wrcc.dri.edu/nps and at ftp://ftp.wrcc.dri.edu/nps/photodocumentation.pdf.

The main purpose for climate stations is to *track climatic conditions through time*. Anything that affects the interpretation of records through time must to be noted and recorded for posterity. The important factors should be clear to a person who has never visited the site, no matter how long ago the site was installed.

In regions with significant, climatic transition zones, transects are an efficient way to span several climates and make use of available resources. Discussions on this topic at greater detail can be found in Redmond and Simeral (2004) and in Redmond et al. (2005).

D.4. Literature Cited

American Association of State Climatologists. 1985. Heights and exposure standards for sensors on automated weather stations. The State Climatologist **9**.

Brock, F. V., K. C. Crawford, R. L. Elliott, G. W. Cuperus, S. J. Stadler, H. L. Johnson and M. D. Eilts. 1995. The Oklahoma Mesonet: A technical overview. Journal of Atmospheric and Oceanic Technology **12**:5-19.

Daly, C., R. P. Neilson, and D. L. Phillips. 1994. A statistical-topographic model for mapping climatological precipitation over mountainous terrain. Journal of Applied Meteorology **33**:140-158.

Daly, C., W. P. Gibson, G. H. Taylor, G. L. Johnson, and P. Pasteris. 2002. A knowledge-based approach to the statistical mapping of climate. Climate Research **22**:99-113.

Doggett, M., C. Daly, J. Smith, W. Gibson, G. Taylor, G. Johnson, and P. Pasteris. 2004. High-resolution 1971-2000 mean monthly temperature maps for the western United States. Fourteenth AMS Conf. on Applied Climatology, 84th AMS Annual Meeting. Seattle, WA, American Meteorological Society, Boston, MA, January 2004, Paper 4.3, CD-ROM.

Geiger, R., R. H. Aron, and P. E. Todhunter. 2003. The Climate Near the Ground. 6th edition. Rowman & Littlefield Publishers, Inc., New York.

Gibson, W. P., C. Daly, T. Kittel, D. Nychka, C. Johns, N. Rosenbloom, A. McNab, and G. Taylor. 2002. Development of a 103-year high-resolution climate data set for the conterminous United States. Thirteenth AMS Conf. on Applied Climatology. Portland, OR, American Meteorological Society, Boston, MA, May 2002:181-183.

Goodison, B. E., P. Y. T. Louie, and D. Yang. 1998. WMO solid precipitation measurement intercomparison final report. WMO TD 982, World Meteorological Organization, Geneva, Switzerland.

National Research Council. 1998. Future of the National Weather Service Cooperative Weather Network. National Academies Press, Washington, D.C.

National Research Council. 2001. A Climate Services Vision: First Steps Toward the Future. National Academies Press, Washington, D.C.

Redmond, K. T. 1992. Effects of observation time on interpretation of climatic time series - A need for consistency. Eighth Annual Pacific Climate (PACLIM) Workshop. Pacific Grove, CA, March 1991:141-150.

Redmond, K. T. 2004. Photographic documentation of long-term climate stations. Available from ftp://ftp.wrcc.dri.edu/nps/photodocumentation.pdf. (accessed 15 August 2004)

Redmond, K. T. and D. B. Simeral. 2004. Climate monitoring comments: Central Alaska Network Inventory and Monitoring Program. Available from ftp://ftp.wrcc.dri.edu/nps/alaska/cakn/npscakncomments040406.pdf. (accessed 6 April 2004)

Redmond, K. T., D. B. Simeral, and G. D. McCurdy. 2005. Climate monitoring for southwest Alaska national parks: network design and site selection. Report 05-01. Western Regional Climate Center, Reno, Nevada.

Redmond, K. T., and G. D. McCurdy. 2005. Channel Islands National Park: Design considerations for weather and climate monitoring. Report 05-02. Western Regional Climate Center, Reno, Nevada.

Sevruk, B., and W. R. Hamon. 1984. International comparison of national precipitation gauges with a reference pit gauge. Instruments and Observing Methods, Report No 17, WMO/TD – 38, World Meteorological Organization, Geneva, Switzerland.

Simpson, J. J., Hufford, G. L., C. Daly, J. S. Berg, and M. D. Fleming. 2005. Comparing maps of mean monthly surface temperature and precipitation for Alaska and adjacent areas of Canada produced by two different methods. Arctic **58**:137-161.

Whiteman, C. D. 2000. Mountain Meteorology: Fundamentals and Applications. Oxford University Press, Oxford, UK.

Wilson, E. O. 1998. Consilience: The Unity of Knowledge. Knopf, New York.

World Meteorological Organization. 1983. Guide to meteorological instruments and methods of observation, No. 8, 5th edition, World Meteorological Organization, Geneva Switzerland.

World Meteorological Organization. 2005. Organization and planning of intercomparisons of rainfall intensity gauges. World Meteorological Organization, Geneva Switzerland.

Yang, D., B. E. Goodison, J. R. Metcalfe, V. S. Golubev, R. Bates, T. Pangburn, and C. Hanson. 1998. Accuracy of NWS 8" standard nonrecording precipitation gauge: results and application of WMO intercomparison. Journal of Atmospheric and Oceanic Technology **15**:54-68.

Yang, D., B. E. Goodison, J. R. Metcalfe, P. Louie, E. Elomaa, C. Hanson, V. Bolubev, T. Gunther, J. Milkovic, and M. Lapin. 2001. Compatibility evaluation of national precipitation gauge measurements. Journal of Geophysical Research **106**:1481-1491.

Appendix E. Master metadata field list

Field Name	Field Type	Field Description
begin_date	date	Effective beginning date for a record.
begin_date_flag	char(2)	Flag describing the known accuracy of the begin date for a station.
best_elevation	float(4)	Best known elevation for a station (in feet).
clim_div_code	char(2)	Foreign key defining climate division code (primary in table: clim_div).
clim_div_key	int2	Foreign key defining climate division for a station (primary in table: clim_div.
clim_div_name	varchar(30)	English name for a climate division.
controller_info	varchar(50)	Person or organization who maintains the identifier system for a given weather or climate network.
country_key	int2	Foreign key defining country where a station resides (primary in table: none).
county_key	int2	Foreign key defining county where a station resides (primary in table: county).
county_name	varchar(31)	English name for a county.
description	text	Any description pertaining to the particular table.
end_date	date	Last effective date for a record.
end_date_flag	char(2)	Flag describing the known accuracy of station end date.
fips_country_code	char(2)	FIPS (federal information processing standards) country code.
fips_state_abbr	char(2)	FIPS state abbreviation for a station.
fips_state_code	char(2)	FIPS state code for a station.
history_flag	char(2)	Describes temporal significance of an individual record among others from the same station.
id_type_key	int2	Foreign key defining the id_type for a station (usually defined in code).
last_updated	date	Date of last update for a record.
latitude	float(8)	Latitude value.
longitude	float(8)	Longitude value.
name_type_key	int2	"3": COOP station name, "2": best station name.
name	varchar(30)	Station name as known at date of last update entry.
ncdc_state_code	char(2)	NCDC, two-character code identifying U.S. state.
network_code	char(8)	Eight-character abbreviation code identifying a network.
network_key	int2	Foreign key defining the network for a station (primary in table: network).
network_station_id	int4	Identifier for a station in the associated network, which is defined by id_type_key.
remark	varchar(254)	Additional information for a record.
src_quality_code	char(2)	Code describing the data quality for the data source.
state_key	int2	Foreign key defining the U.S. state where a station resides (primary in table: state).
state_name	varchar(30)	English name for a state.
station_alt_name	varchar(30)	Other English names for a station.
station_best_name	varchar(30)	Best, most well-known English name for a station.
time_zone	float4	Time zone where a station resides.
ucan_station_id	int4	Unique station identifier for every station in ACIS.
unit_key	int2	Integer value representing a unit of measure.

Field Name	Field Type	Field Description
updated_by	char(8)	Person who last updated a record.
var_major_id	int2	Defines major climate variable.
var_minor_id	int2	Defines data source within a var_major_id.
zipcode	char(5)	Zipcode where a latitude/longitude point resides.
nps_netcode	char(4)	Network four-character identifier.
nps_netname	varchar(128)	Displayed English name for a network.
parkcode	char(4)	Park four-character identifier.
parkname	varchar(128)	Displayed English name for a park/
im_network	char(4)	NPS I&M network where park belongs (a net code)/
station_id	varchar(16)	Station identifier.
station_id_type	varchar(16)	Type of station identifier.
network.subnetwork.id	varchar(16)	Identifier of a sub-network in associated network.
subnetwork_key	int2	Foreign key defining sub-network for a station.
subnetwork_name	varchar(30)	English name for a sub-network.
slope	integer	Terrain slope at the location.
aspect	integer	Terrain aspect at the station.
gps	char(1)	Indicator of latitude/longitude recorded via GPS.
site_description	text(0)	Physical description of site.
route_directions	text(0)	Driving route or site access directions.
station_photo_id	integer	Unique identifier associating a group of photos to a station. Group of photos all taken on same date.
photo_id	char(30)	Unique identifier for a photo.
photo_date	datetime	Date photograph taken.
photographer	varchar(64)	Name of photographer.
maintenance_date	datetime	Date of station maintenance visit.
contact_key	Integer	Unique identifier associating contact information to a station.
full_name	varchar(64)	Full name of contact person.
organization	varchar(64)	Organization of contact person.
contact_type	varchar(32)	Type of contact person (operator, administrator, etc.)
position_title	varchar(32)	Title of contact person.
address	varchar(32)	Address for contact person.
city	varchar(32)	City for contact person.
state	varchar(2)	State for contact person.
zip_code	char(10)	Zipcode for contact person.
country	varchar(32)	Country for contact person.
email	varchar(64)	E-mail for contact person.
work_phone	varchar(16)	Work phone for contact person.
contact_notes	text(254)	Other details regarding contact person.
equipment_type	char(30)	Sensor measurement type; i.e., wind speed, air temperature, etc.
eq_manufacturer	char(30)	Manufacturer of equipment.
eq_model	char(20)	Model number of equipment.
serial_num	char(20)	Serial number of equipment.
eq_description	varchar(254)	Description of equipment.
install_date	datetime	Installation date of equipment.
remove_date	datetime	Removal date of equipment.
ref_height	integer	Sensor displacement height from surface.
sampling_interval	varchar(10)	Frequency of sensor measurement.

Appendix F. Electronic supplements

F.1. ACIS metadata file for weather and climate stations associated with the CHDN:
http://www.wrcc.dri.edu/nps/pub/CHDN/metadata/CHDN_from_ACIS.tar.gz.

Appendix G. Descriptions of weather/climate monitoring networks

G.1. Clean Air Status and Trends Network (CASTNet)

- Purpose of network: provide information for evaluating the effectiveness of national emission-control strategies.
- Primary management agency: EPA.
- Data website: http://epa.gov/castnet/.
- Measured weather/climate elements:
  o Air temperature.
  o Precipitation.
  o Relative humidity.
  o Wind speed.
  o Wind direction.
  o Wind gust.
  o Gust direction.
  o Solar radiation.
  o Soil moisture and temperature.
- Sampling frequency: hourly.
- Reporting frequency: hourly.
- Estimated station cost: $13000.
- Network strengths:
  o High-quality data.
  o Sites are well maintained.
- Network weaknesses:
  o Density of station coverage is low.
  o Shorter periods of record for western U.S.

The CASTNet network is primarily is an air-quality-monitoring network managed by the EPA. The elements shown here are intended to support interpretation of measured air-quality parameters such as ozone, nitrates, sulfides, etc., which also are measured at CASTNet sites.

G.2. NWS Cooperative Observer Program (COOP)

- Purpose of network:
  o Provide observational, meteorological data required to define U.S. climate and help measure long-term climate changes.
  o Provide observational, meteorological data in near real-time to support forecasting and warning mechanisms and other public service programs of the NWS.
- Primary management agency: NOAA (NWS).
- Data website: data are available from the NCDC (http://www.ncdc.noaa.gov), RCCs (e.g., WRCC, http://www.wrcc.dri.edu), and state climate offices.
- Measured weather/climate elements:
  o Maximum, minimum, and observation-time temperature.
  o Precipitation, snowfall, snow depth.

- o Pan evaporation (some stations).
- Sampling frequency: daily.
- Reporting frequency: daily or monthly (station-dependent).
- Estimated station cost: $2000 with maintenance costs of $500–900/year.
- Network strengths:
  - o Decade–century records at most sites.
  - o Widespread national coverage (thousands of stations).
  - o Excellent data quality when well maintained.
  - o Relatively inexpensive; highly cost effective.
  - o Manual measurements; not automated.
- Network weaknesses:
  - o Uneven exposures; many are not well-maintained.
  - o Dependence on schedules for volunteer observers.
  - o Slow entry of data from many stations into national archives.
  - o Data subject to observational methodology; not always documented.
  - o Manual measurements; not automated and not hourly.

The COOP network has long served as the main climate observation network in the U.S. Readings are usually made by volunteers using equipment supplied, installed, and maintained by the federal government. The observer in effect acts as a host for the data-gathering activities and supplies the labor; this is truly a "cooperative" effort. The SAO sites often are considered to be part of the cooperative network as well if they collect the previously mentioned types of weather/climate observations. Typical observation days are morning to morning, evening to evening, or midnight to midnight. By convention, observations are ascribed to the date the instrument was reset at the end of the observational period. For this reason, midnight observations represent the end of a day. The Historical Climate Network is a subset of the cooperative network but contains longer and more complete records.

G.3. Citizen Weather Observer Program (CWOP)

- Purpose of network: collect observations from private citizens and make these data available for homeland security and other weather applications, providing constant feedback to the observers to maintain high data quality.
- Primary management agency: NOAA MADIS program.
- Data Website: http://www.wxqa.com.
- Measured weather/climate elements:
  - o Air temperature.
  - o Dewpoint temperature.
  - o Precipitation.
  - o Wind speed and direction.
  - o Barometric pressure.
- Sampling frequency: 15 minutes or less.
- Reporting frequency: 15 minutes.
- Estimated station cost: unknown.
- Network strengths:
  - o Active partnership between public agencies and private citizens.

o Large number of participant sites.
o Regular communications between data providers and users, encouraging higher data quality.
- Network weaknesses:
o Variable instrumentation platforms.
o Metadata are sometimes limited.

The CWOP network is a public-private partnership with U.S. citizens and various agencies including NOAA, NASA (National Aeronautics and Space Administration), and various universities. There are over 4500 registered sites worldwide, with close to 3000 of these sites located in North America.

G.4. NPS Gaseous Pollutant Monitoring Program (GPMP)

- Purpose of network: measurement of ozone and related meteorological elements.
- Primary management agency: NPS.
- Data website: http://www2.nature.nps.gov/air/monitoring.
- Measured weather/climate elements:
o Air temperature.
o Relative humidity.
o Precipitation.
o Wind speed and direction.
o Solar radiation.
o Surface wetness.
- Sampling frequency: continuous.
- Reporting frequency: hourly.
- Estimated station cost: unknown.
- Network strengths:
o Stations are located within NPS park units.
o Data quality is excellent, with high data standards.
o Provides unique measurements that are not available elsewhere.
o Records are up to 2 decades in length.
o Site maintenance is excellent.
o Thermometers are aspirated.
- Network weaknesses:
o Not easy to download the entire data set or to ingest live data.
o Period of record is short compared to other automated networks. Earliest sites date from 2004.
o Station spacing and coverage: station installation is episodic, driven by opportunistic situations.

The NPS web site indicates that there are 33 sites with continuous ozone analysis run by NPS, with records from a few to about 16-17 years. Of these stations, 12 are labeled as GPMP sites and the rest are labeled as CASTNet sites. All of these have standard meteorological measurements, including a 10-m mast. Another nine GPMP sites are located within NPS units but run by cooperating agencies. A number of other sites (1-2 dozen) ran for differing periods in the past, generally less than 5-10 years.

G.5. NOAA Ground-Based GPS Meteorology (GPS-MET) Network

- Purpose of network:
  - o Measure atmospheric water vapor using ground-based GPS receivers.
  - o Facilitate use of these data operational and in other research and applications.
  - o Provides data for weather forecasting, atmospheric modeling and prediction, climate monitoring, calibrating and validation other observing systems including radiosondes and satellites, and research.
- Primary management agency: NOAA Earth System Research Laboratory.
- Data website: http://gpsmet.noaa.gov/jsp/index.jsp.
- Measurements:
  - o Dual frequency carrier phase measurements every 30 seconds.
- Ancillary weather/climate observations:
  - o Air temperature.
  - o Relative humidity.
  - o Pressure.
- Reporting frequency: currently 30 min.
- Estimated station cost: $0-$10000, depending on approach. Data from dual frequency GPS receivers installed for conventional applications (e.g. high accuracy surveying) can be used without modification.
- Network strengths:
  - o Frequent, high-quality measurements.
  - o High reliability.
  - o All-weather operability.
  - o Many uses.
  - o Highly leveraged.
  - o Requires no calibration.
  - o Measurement accuracy improves with time.
- Network weakness:
  - o Point measurement.
  - o Provides no direct information about the vertical distribution of water vapor.

The GPS-MET network is the first network of its kind dedicated to GPS meteorology (see Duan et al. 1996). The GPS-MET network was developed in response to the need for improved moisture observations to support weather forecasting, climate monitoring, and other research activities. GPS-MET is a collaboration between NOAA and several other governmental and university organizations and institutions.

GPS meteorology utilizes the radio signals broadcast by the satellite Global Positioning System for atmospheric remote sensing. GPS meteorology applications have evolved along two paths: ground-based (Bevis et al. 1992) and space-based (Yuan et al. 1993). Both applications make the same fundamental measurement (the apparent delay in the arrival of radio signals caused by changes in the radio-refractivity of the atmosphere along the paths of the radio signals) but they do so from different perspectives.

In ground-based GPS meteorology, a GPS receiver and antenna are placed at a fixed location on the ground and the signals from all GPS satellites in view are continuously recorded. From this information, the exact position of the GPS antenna can be determined over time with high (millimeter-level) accuracy. Subsequent measurements of the antenna position are compared with the known position, and the differences can be attributed to changes in the temperature, pressure and water vapor in the atmosphere above the antenna. By making continuous measurements of temperature and pressure at the site, the total amount of water vapor in the atmosphere at this location can be estimated with high accuracy under all weather conditions. For more information on ground based GPS meteorology the reader is referred to http://gpsmet.noaa.gov.

In space-based GPS meteorology, GPS receivers and antennas are placed on satellites in Low Earth Orbit (LEO), and the signals transmitted by a GPS satellite are continuously recorded as a GPS satellite "rises" or "sets" behind the limb of the Earth. This process is called an occultation or a limb sounding. The GPS radio signals bend more as they encounter a thicker atmosphere and the bending (which causes an apparent increase in the length of the path of the radio signal) can be attributed to changes in temperature, pressure and water vapor along the path of the radio signal through the atmosphere that is nominally about 300 km long. The location of an occultation depends on the relative geometries of the GPS satellites in Mid Earth Orbit and the satellites in LEO. As a consequence, information about the vertical temperature, pressure and moisture structure of the Earth's atmosphere as a whole can be estimated with high accuracy, but not at any one particular place over time. The main difference between ground and space-based GPS meteorology is one of geometry. A space-based measurement can be thought of as a ground-based measurement turned on its side. For more information on space based GPS meteorology, the reader is referred to http://www.cosmic.ucar.edu/gpsmet/.

G.6. National Atmospheric Deposition Program (NADP)

- Purpose of network: measurement of precipitation chemistry and atmospheric deposition.
- Primary management agencies: USDA, but multiple collaborators.
- Data website: http://nadp.sws.uiuc.edu.
- Measured weather/climate elements:
  o Precipitation.
- Sampling frequency: daily.
- Reporting frequency: daily.
- Estimated station cost: unknown.
- Network strengths:
  o Data quality is excellent, with high data standards.
  o Site maintenance is excellent.
- Network weaknesses:
  o A very limited number of climate parameters are measured.

Stations within the NADP network monitor primarily wet deposition through precipitation chemistry at selected sites around the U.S. and its territories. The network is a collaborative effort among several agencies including USGS and USDA. Precipitation is the primary climate parameter measured at NADP sites. This network includes MDN sites.

G.7. Remote Automated Weather Station Network (RAWS)

- Purpose of network: provide near-real-time (hourly or near hourly) measurements of meteorological variables for use in fire weather forecasts and climatology. Data from RAWS also are used for natural resource management, flood forecasting, natural hazard management, and air-quality monitoring.
- Primary management agency: WRCC, National Interagency Fire Center.
- Data website: http://www.raws.dri.edu/index.html.
- Measured weather/climate elements:
  o Air temperature.
  o Precipitation.
  o Relative humidity.
  o Wind speed.
  o Wind direction.
  o Wind gust.
  o Gust direction.
  o Solar radiation.
  o Soil moisture and temperature.
- Sampling frequency: 1 or 10 minutes, element-dependent.
- Reporting frequency: generally hourly. Some stations report every 15 or 30 minutes.
- Estimated station cost: $12000 with satellite telemetry ($8000 without satellite telemetry); maintenance costs are around $2000/year.
- Network strengths:
  o Metadata records are usually complete.
  o Sites are located in remote areas.
  o Sites are generally well-maintained.
  o Entire period of record available on-line.
- Network weaknesses:
  o RAWS network is focused largely on fire management needs (formerly focused only on fire needs).
  o Frozen precipitation is not measured reliably.
  o Station operation is not always continuous.
  o Data transmission is completed via one-way telemetry. Data are therefore recoverable either in real-time or not at all.

The RAWS network is used by many land-management agencies, such as the BLM, NPS, Fish and Wildlife Service, Bureau of Indian Affairs, Forest Service, and other agencies. The RAWS network was one of the first automated weather station networks to be installed in the U.S. Most gauges do not have heaters, so hydrologic measurements are of little value when temperatures dip below freezing or reach freezing after frozen precipitation events. There are approximately 1100 real-time sites in this network and about 1800 historic sites (some are decommissioned or

85

moved). The sites can transmit data all winter but may be in deep snow in some locations. The WRCC is the archive for this network and receives station data and metadata through a special connection to the National Interagency Fire Center in Boise, Idaho.

G.8. NWS/FAA Surface Airways Observation Network (SAO)

- Purpose of network: provide near-real-time (hourly or near hourly) measurements of meteorological variables and are used both for airport operations and weather forecasting.
- Primary management agency: NOAA, FAA.
- Data website: data are available from state climate offices, RCCs (e.g., WRCC, http://www.wrcc.dri.edu), and NCDC (http://www.ncdc.noaa.gov).
- Measured weather/climate elements:
  o Air temperature.
  o Dewpoint and/or relative humidity.
  o Wind speed.
  o Wind direction.
  o Wind gust.
  o Gust direction.
  o Barometric pressure.
  o Precipitation (not at many FAA sites).
  o Sky cover.
  o Ceiling (cloud height).
  o Visibility.
- Sampling frequency: element-dependent.
- Reporting frequency: element-dependent.
- Estimated station cost: $100000–$200000, with maintenance costs approximately $10000/year.
- Network strengths:
  o Records generally extend over several decades.
  o Consistent maintenance and station operations.
  o Data record is reasonably complete and usually high quality.
  o Hourly or sub-hourly data.
- Network weaknesses:
  o Nearly all sites are located at airports.
  o Data quality can be related to size of airport—smaller airports tend to have poorer datasets.
  o Influences from urbanization and other land-use changes.

These stations are managed by NOAA, U. S. Navy, U. S. Air Force, and FAA. These stations are located generally at major airports and military bases. The FAA stations often do not record precipitation, or they may provide precipitation records of reduced quality. Automated stations are typically ASOSs for the NWS or AWOSs for the FAA. Some sites only report episodically with observers paid per observation.

G.9. Weather For You Network (WX4U)

- Purpose of network: allow volunteer weather enthusiasts around the U.S. to observe and share weather data.
- Data website: http://www.met.utah.edu/jhorel/html/mesonet.
- Measured weather/climate elements:
  o Air temperature.
  o Relative humidity and dewpoint temperature.
  o Precipitation.
  o Wind speed and direction.
  o Wind gust and direction.
  o Barometric pressure.
- Sampling frequency: 10 minutes.
- Reporting frequency: 10 minutes.
- Estimated station cost: unknown.
- Network strengths:
  o Stations are located throughout the U.S.
  o Stations provide near-real-time observations.
- Network weaknesses:
  o Instrumentation platforms can be variable.
  o Data are sometimes of questionable quality.

The WX4U network is a nationwide collection of weather stations run by local observers. Meteorological elements that are measured usually include temperature, precipitation, wind, and humidity.

NPS/CHDN/NRTR—2007/034, May 2007